CRASHING
THE OLD BOYS'
NETWORK

Lake Superior College Library

CRASHING THE OLD BOYS' NETWORK

The Tragedies and Triumphs of Girls and Women in Sports

David F. Salter

PRAEGER

Westport, Connecticut
London

Library of Congress Cataloging-in-Publication Data

Salter, David F.
    Crashing the old boys' network : the tragedies and triumphs of
girls and women in sports / David F. Salter.
        p.   cm.
    Includes bibliographical references (p.   ) and index.
    ISBN 0–275–95512–5 (alk. paper)
    1. Women athletes.   2. Sports for women.   3. Sex discrimination in
sports.   I. Title.
GV709.S32   1996
796'.0194—dc20   96–10427

British Library Cataloguing in Publication Data is available.

Copyright © 1996 by David F. Salter

All rights reserved. No portion of this book may be
reproduced, by any process or technique, without the
express written consent of the publisher.

Library of Congress Catalog Card Number: 96–10427
ISBN: 0–275–95512–5

First published in 1996

Praeger Publishers, 88 Post Road West, Westport, CT 06881
An imprint of Greenwood Publishing Group, Inc.

Printed in the United States of America

The paper used in this book complies with the
Permanent Paper Standard issued by the National
Information Standards Organization (Z39.48–1984).

10 9 8 7 6 5 4 3 2

To Katy and Emily:
> You can accomplish anything you set your minds to.

Contents

Acknowledgments

It is rare that a major undertaking is accomplished by a single individual. In life, as in sports, victories are rarely achieved without the efforts of many players. Teamwork is critical for successful achievement.

This project would not have been possible without the valuable contributions of many people. I am grateful to those who shared their experiences with sincerity, candor, and honesty. While an author has his name on a book, this story is not my story. This story belongs to fathers, mothers and daughters, coaches, administrators, and the pioneers and guardians of girls and women in sports.

I am particularly struck by the willingness of so many people to enlighten and educate a curious writer. This varied from Daedra Charles and Bridgette Gordon who spoke with me at midnight, Italian time, which was a reasonable time here in the States, to Lesley Visser, who called me from Chicago during a whirlwind Thanksgiving week during which she visited five cities in six days.

This cooperation not only provided a strong foundation for this project, but instilled confidence in an anxious author and confirmed his belief in the value of his vision. My heartfelt thanks go to the following, as well as to those behind the scenes, who handled important tasks that often go unnoticed.

Susan True	Ann Meyers	Carol Blazejowski
Ken Dempsey	Daedra Charles	Bridgette Gordon

Mary Alice Hill	Billie Jean King	Dennis M. Sullivan
Jackson Katz	John Korff	Tracey Donnelly
Richard Lapchick	James Fuhse	Renee Bloch Shallouf
Donna Lopiano	Ty Votaw	Toni Waters Woods
Sandra Scott, Ph.D.	Suzyn Waldman	Jill Jeffrey
Joanne Austin	Robin Roberts	Maureen Coyle
Dorothy McIntyre	Lesley Visser	Timothy Stoner
Kathryn M. Reith	Nanci Donnellan	Robin Finn
Summer Sanders	Chris Berman	Pat Head Summitt
Skip Colcord	John Walsh	Mary Joe Fernandez
Christine Grant, Ph.D.	Cheryl Levick	Jody Conradt
Marilyn McNeil	Cathy Henkel	Lisa Raymond
Jane Miller	Jody Goldstein	Betty Jaynes
Merrily Dean Baker	Anne Gillespie-Lewis	James Haluck
Constance Hurlbut	Rachel Shuster	

Special thanks go to Dave Nagle, Chris LaPlaca, Linda Recant, Rosa Gatti in the ESPN Communications Department, David Kellis, and the folks at Creamer, Dickson, Basford.

As this book will show, parental support is critical for children. That support has no limits, even when a child reaches adulthood. Mom and Dad always told me I could accomplish anything I set my mind to. This book tells me that motto is still true. Special thanks to my mom who dedicated countless hours to transcribing miles of audio tape from the many interviews that were conducted.

Joe Valenzano promised me he would find a publisher for my project, and he never relented until he found us a home at the Greenwood Publishing Group. Thanks Joe. Thanks to Lynn Taylor and the rest of the folks at Greenwood, who not only saw the value of this project, but were willing to make the commitment to produce this work.

Finally, thanks to Diane, my best friend and lifelong partner, and our daughters, Katy and Emily. You enlighten me every day.

Introduction

When does a person become enlightened? How does the illumination oc-cur? I can't be a hypocrite. It took me many years to feel enlightened, and I know I have not fully arrived at that stage. It is a daily process, and many times, it is a struggle.

Growing up in a middle-class family of Italian/German descent instilled in me many important values. Although some would view those values as old fashioned, I embrace them, but I also recognize that some of those beliefs were unfounded.

Like many young boys growing up in the 1960s and 1970s, everyday pickup games were the Super Bowl, the World Series, or the NBA Cham-pionship—even if it was really just for the bragging rights of Kimberly Road. All the guys in the neighborhood got together every day and com-peted from sunup to sundown in a rotating frenzy of wiffle ball, touch football, and driveway basketball. Girls were not allowed.

Nor did we even consider there might be some who wanted to join our free-for-all. After all, the girl's part was to be the cheerleader, replete with pom-poms, short skirts, letter sweaters, and those funky white shoes with the black dog ear on each side. Girls weren't athletes. They weren't sup-posed to be. Sweating was very un-ladylike. Even their participation in gym class was nothing more than the fulfillment of an educational requirement. Girls certainly couldn't perform great feats of strength, speed, and agility.

High school athletics did nothing to alter these perceptions. While we did have a number of strong girls' teams, sold-out crowds were reserved for the football team on Saturday afternoons, not for the state championship field hockey team. Boys' teams received top-of-the-line equipment and never had an unmet need. I can't really recall whether the girls' teams had what they needed or not. At that time, it wasn't something a teenage boy spent much time contemplating.

Ironically, some of my most enduring memories of athletic events during those years are of Chris Evert's battles with Martina Navratilova at Wimbledon or the French Open, the U.S. women figure skaters and the Romanian gymnasts in the Olympics, and Billie Jean King's sound defeat of Bobby Riggs in the infamous battle of the sexes at the Houston Astrodome.

College athletics reaffirmed the opinions I had carried with me through high school. College football was the primary focus of the athletic department as far as many were concerned. Men's basketball was a close second. Women's sports were virtually invisible. We knew they were there, somewhere. We just rarely saw them, and even more uncommon was actually hearing anything about any of the women's teams. Reflecting on the coaches and administrators involved in that athletic department, it is difficult to believe that those people would consciously ignore the women student-athletes. My days as a college student-athlete occurred, however, during the same time period that Grove City College was involved in a legal battle with the U.S. government over the specificity of Title IX and its application to an intercollegiate athletic program. That Federal law stated simply that no person could be discriminated against, on the basis of sex, under any education program or activity receiving Federal financial assistance. Grove City's court victory, temporary as it was, perpetuated the Neanderthal thought process. Enlightenment was elusive.

As women began earning more visibility in the electronic media in the early 1980s, men were given another reason to dislike women in sports. Not only were girls and women beginning to participate more frequently and in greater numbers, now they also wanted to *tell* guys about sports. What a contradiction in terms. Guys and sports were synonymous. How could a female report on a football game? As ESPN's Lesley Visser recalls, "Women in the sports media were thought to be from Mars."

Marriage and children can enlighten a man in a hurry, especially when his children are daughters whom he loves like nothing else on the planet. As gender equity became a burning topic in athletics, the painstaking research process took place. The more information that was gathered and examined and the more coaches, administrators, and athletes who were interviewed, the more the intensity grew. I thought, "If there is anyone who thinks my daughters will be denied fair and equitable treatment, they are going to have one angry, vocal, and resourceful father to deal with."

That was my thought, and it hasn't changed. My hope was, and still is, that other fathers would join the crusade because, as we approach the year 2000, nearly twenty-five years after the passage of Title IX, girls and women in sports are still fighting an uphill battle. It is unbelievable that in 1996 girls and women in sports remain challenged by antiquated beliefs and by an athletics system that is reluctant to change and continues to subdue equitable advances. Enlightenment is not universal.

1

Still Struggling

Until we convince John Q. Public that girls have the same right and need for the athletic experience as boys do, you won't have enough public outcry.

—Susan True, Assistant Director,
National Federation of State High School Associations

Mary Alice Hill didn't know that being blackballed would hurt so much, nor did she know what it would cost her. Becoming the first woman ever to be named athletic director at an NCAA Division I university had a price.

Hill was named acting director of athletics at San Diego State in 1980 and had the term "acting" removed from her title in 1982. After completing many of the tasks the university asked of her when she assumed the role—increase fund-raising, operate a balanced budget, increase ticket sales, acquire corporate sponsorship—Hill was fired by San Diego State president Tom Day in 1985 for no concrete reason. Hill, like many other women in collegiate athletics today, was on a year-to-year contract, and so it was convenient for Day to terminate her with the simple justification that he had "lost confidence" in her.

But there is more substance to that story than Day would like anyone to know. Ten years later, Hill would easily have won a sex discrimination suit against her employer. In 1985, however, after she had been through one successful, but grueling, court case with Colorado State, Hill's legal battle with San Diego State turned into a dead end.

Hill's collegiate administrative career started as women's athletic director at Colorado State in 1972, the first year Title IX was passed. As with most women's administrative positions, she also taught courses, coached women's track and field, and was director of intramurals. At that time, the women's athletic program at the Fort Collins institution was budgeted for $5,500 per year, whereas the men's athletic program was receiving $1.4 million. Hill was asked to create a budget for the women's program, which had never been done. When Hill developed a budget stressing equality between the men's and women's programs, the chairman of the Physical Education Department, Hill's boss, dismissed the proposal.

"He just laughed and said this is ridiculous, we can't do this," Hill explained. "I asked him if he minded if I took it to the president of the university, and he said, 'Of course not.' The president thought it was wonderful and put together a task force to bring in more money for the women's program. It really threatened the folks there and so they went about finding a way to get rid of me."

The official reason CSU gave for terminating Hill was failure to comply with a condition in her contract that stipulated she agreed to go back to graduate school to attain an advanced degree. But that clause never existed.

"No, no, no, there was no prior agreement," Hill stated. "In fact, on my personal evaluation form, prior to my going to the president with my budget proposal, my evaluation was glowing and wonderful. And there was no mention of an advanced degree. There was even a place in the contract for them to include that clause, and they didn't."

After what Hill calls a "long, arduous" court case, because it was a trial by jury, she won the lawsuit and damages were awarded. The case, however, did not deter San Diego State's athletic director, Ken Karr, from hiring Hill in 1976 as associate director for women's athletics and women's track and field coach.

"I asked Ken, 'Are you threatened by someone like me who went to court with the university,' and he said, 'No, that is one of the reasons I hired you.' Ken was wonderful because he included me in everything that happened at San Diego State. The very first meeting I was involved in, San Diego State was hosting the University of Miami in a football game. There were going to be 62,000 people there and the largest event I had ever been involved in drew maybe 600 people. It was incredibly educational for me."

According to Hill, Karr was not in favor with the president of the institution, and the president moved Karr out of the athletic director position and into another area. Hill filled in on an interim basis before Cedric Dempsey took over. Hill indicated Dempsey fell out of favor with the president, also, and he was off to the University of Houston after just three months at San Diego State. The likely choice to replace Dempsey was already at the institution, but the president was not quite ready to acknowledge that fact.

"The president called me in and said, 'You know Mary, you are ready for this job as athletic director,' " Hill recalled. " 'I know you are ready for this job because you have done a great job here and people respect you. You should have a splendid opportunity to really see what you can do in fund-raising, because you haven't had a chance to do that. I would like to put you in this position, but I can't,' the president continued. 'I feel the community wouldn't be able to handle a woman in this position. So what I am going to do is hire a man and I am going to make you associate director for both men and women.' "

"The president told me he wanted me to get more involved in fund-raising, and I asked him how long this would be, this was 1978. He said two or three years. So I went through that role for three years and became extremely involved in everything the department was doing. I also became involved on the NCAA Council."

Gene Templeton, the person hired to replace Dempsey, had a heart attack, and again Hill was thrust into the 'acting' director position. At that point, other institutions began to contact Hill about open positions in their athletic departments, and Hill was eager to pursue those positions. When Hill approached the president, he did not discourage her from following the leads, but didn't appear to want to lose Hill, either. Two days later, he came back and offered Hill the athletic director's position, but with conditions.

"He said, 'Gene has decided to take early retirement, and I am going to name you Athletic Director,' " Hill remembered. " 'Acting athletic director, because I have to find out for myself what the community will think about you. You have all the skills that are necessary, but I just want to see what the community will do. And I must tell you I am doing this against the advice of all of my vice presidents. They don't think you belong in that position because you are too strong a person and will not do what we ask of you.' "

At this point, according to Hill, she began to implement approximately thirty new programs for the athletic department, including balancing the budget, which had not been done in the previous seven or eight years. The Aztecs had lost about 9,000 season ticket holders for football because of a seating priority mishap, and Hill revived about 6,000 of those patrons. Hill enticed corporate sponsors to endorse some of the coaching positions, so that those positions were no longer a drain on the budget.

After several stints as "acting" athletic director in parts of 1980 and 1981, Hill finally became athletic director in 1982. Unfortunately, her tenure would not last long. In the midst of Dempsey's departure, Hill had filed paperwork to increase all the salaries of the women's coaches to levels comparable to those of the men's coaches. The university did not "catch" this request for approximately six months, according to Hill. Obviously this did not sit well with the administration. "The president wanted me to pull the money away from them [the women's coaches] and I told him I could not do that," Hill said.

Hill continued to enhance and battle for women's athletics, to fight against the double standards she claims existed for minority athletes in football and men's basketball, and to engage in other, similar battles until the president called her in in 1985 and told her he had lost confidence in her and was terminating her.

After serving nine years at San Diego State in a variety of capacities, four years at Colorado State, and four years on the NCAA Council, as well as terms on the NCAA Eligibility Committee and the NCAA Television Negotiations Committee, Hill couldn't get a sniff at a job, not even an interview.

"I don't know if I should use the term blackball," Hill hesitated. "They are an old boys' network that is very effective. This is true. I have applied for more than 200 positions in collegiate athletics, from athletic director, to associate, to assistant on all three levels: Divisions I, II, and III. If you look at my resumé and know my credentials, there has got to be a reason why I was not even getting invited in for interviews. Before I was fired at San Diego State, people from other institutions were calling me to apply for jobs, and then it was like no one had ever heard of me."

It is ironic because competent people lose their jobs every day and then earn a position with another company. Dismissals often occur for the simplest reasons, such as a conflict of personalities. But Hill was the first woman athletic director hired at a Division I institution and the first woman fired, as well.

Karr, after being reassigned by Day, later left and was hired as the athletic director at North Carolina State. Two and a half years after her departure from San Diego State, Hill contacted Karr to get some advice. Karr told Hill he had asked for and received a letter of recommendation, generic as it was, from Day, and that Hill needed to do the same if she had any hopes of getting back into athletics. Hill wrote a letter to Day asking for the most basic recommendation letter.

"He took about two months and wrote me back and said, 'Yes he had given Ken a letter of recommendation, but in my case he did not feel he could do that,' " Hill said. "He stated he wanted to speak to any schools that contacted him on a case-by-case basis. And I never got that opportunity. I think a lot of schools contacted him without me putting him down as a reference, and that is why I wasn't getting the interviews."

Hill finally developed a training center for thoroughbred horses, and she dabbled in some other areas before she found a home in athletics as executive director of the National Association for Girls and Women in Sport. Hill fortunately finally found a new home, but many similar stories do not have happy endings.

"You've come a long way, Baby." This certainly was a catchy advertising jingle at one time. Although it is not politically correct, its theme is appropriate. Or is it?

Two women are sitting on the Supreme Court; a woman is the U.S. Attorney General; women are occupying positions at the highest levels of politics, business, law, and medicine. A woman (actress Kate Mulgrew) even commands a Star Trek vessel. What would Captain Kirk say? Would Mr. Spock think it "illogical"?

Many people still think it is inappropriate, however, for females to be intensely involved in athletics, be it as a player, coach, or administrator. In this era, when women have made great strides in many other segments of society, women athletes are still an oxymoron—almost. Nearly twenty-five years after the passage of Title IX to the Education Amendments Act of 1972, approximately 90 percent of all colleges and universities in the United States are not in compliance with this federal law. Ironically, there are few laws protecting women in other endeavors similar to the way Title IX was meant to fortify women in athletics. Strangely, it has taken twenty years for a federal law to be enforced. Hopefully it won't take another twenty years to make amends for decades of neglect.

WHAT IS TITLE IX?

In layman's terms, Title IX of the Education Amendments Act of 1972 prohibits sex discrimination in educational institutions that receive federal funds. In brief it states: "No person in the United States shall, on the basis of sex, be excluded from participation in, be denied the benefits of, or be subjected to discrimination under any education program or activity receiving Federal financial assistance."

Although this applies to almost all educational institutions in the United States, statistics show the stark reality. For example, there are only six female athletic directors at NCAA Division I schools, just two of whom are at institutions that play both major revenue-producing sports: football and basketball. There are only two female commissioners of Division I all-sports athletic conferences.

The differences between Divisions I, II, and III are based upon some primary components such as the type of financial aid offered, number of sports sponsored, eligibility requirements, and academic requirements. For example, Division I institutions must sponsor a minimum of fourteen sports, seven each for men and women, while Division II institutions must sponsor a minimum of eight sports, four each for men and women. Division III institutions do not offer athletic scholarships, only financial aid based on need, while Division I and II schools can offer athletic scholarships.

While undergraduate enrollment of men and women in America's colleges and universities is virtually equal, only 32 percent of athletic scholarships are awarded to female student-athletes.[1] According to the NCAA Gender Equity Study (1990), male college student-athletes received approximately $180 million *more* in scholarships every year than female student-athletes.[2] Citing the 1992 NCAA Gender Equity Study, in Division IA, for every dollar spent recruiting female student-athletes, four are spent recruiting male student-athletes.[3]

In the ten years from 1982 to 1992, there was an increase of 812 jobs for coaches of women's teams. Only 180 of those, or 22 percent, were filled by women. Overall, approximately 48 percent of women's NCAA teams are coached by women. In 1972, 90 percent of all NCAA women's teams were coached by women.[4]

In fact, according to the Collegiate Sports Aptitude Test (1992), women have a better chance of becoming a president of their college or university than the athletic director. Overall, at Division I schools, there are fifteen female presidents and eleven female athletic directors; in Division II, twenty-seven female presidents and twenty-three athletic directors; and at Division III institutions, sixty-nine presidents and sixty-five athletic directors.[5]

WHAT'S THE PROBLEM?

In the February 1994 issue of *Playboy*, ESPN sportscaster Chris Berman provided an interesting perspective.

> Women bond in ways that you and I don't understand. They probably had high-level conversations at younger ages than we did. But there is something intrinsic about sports. My playing catch or shooting hoops with my Dad when I was nine doesn't necessarily make me any smarter about sports than a woman. But you sit around with the fellas and watch a ballgame. There is a certain bonding, and maybe sports is a huge reason for it. Most women aren't going to hang around with five other women and watch games on a regular basis. There are some women who have the same intrinsic feelings about sports, but it's a real small number who grew up exactly like I did. With the fervor.[6]

Some will object to Berman's thesis; however, there is truth, significance, and revelation in his words. Berman uncovers some key facts. First, not a point to be overlooked, fathers spend a lot more time playing ball with their sons than with their daughters. Second, a person's gender, in no way, shape, or form can determine one's ability to understand or participate in athletics. Berman also alludes to the fact that men and women view sports with different parameters. This speaks directly to the idea that men and women participate in and obtain satisfaction from athletics in totally different ways. There is nothing wrong with that view.

Let's establish one core belief at the outset. Men and women were created physically different. Now, while an extremist like Gloria Steinem would have you believe this is an evil thing, it's not.

As Women's Sports Foundation executive director Donna Lopiano wrote in a *USA Today* article: "Males have more of the hormone androgen, which allows them to develop more muscle mass per unit volume of body weight. They enjoy a significant physical advantage because most sports are strength, speed, and reaction-time activities."[7]

Physical dissimilarities are not the problem. The problem is the way society has viewed and treated these differences. Men have portrayed physical differences as overall weakness in females, and they have parlayed that perception to gain the dominant course in society. Whether you believe in Creationism, Darwinism, or Lamarckism, the bottom line shows men to have certain physical characteristics that women do not have and vice versa. This is not meant to be a philosophical or religious debate. How does this relate to athletics?

These physical differences might prevent a female from being competitive at the highest level of football or hockey, but they do not preclude a female from participating in a multitude of other competitive sports. That is one of the basic misconceptions about this entire struggle to achieve gender equity. Women do not necessarily want to compete against men or with men. It's about opportunity, or the lack of it. Women are simply striving for an equal opportunity to pursue their athletic interests with the same vigor, enthusiasm, and fervor that Berman talks about.

This is not about Jane Doe's wanting to strap on thirty pounds of football equipment to play middle linebacker for Michigan State in the Rose Bowl. This is about Jane Doe's searching for an opportunity to play for the women's soccer team (if one exists) with equipment, quality coaching, resources, facilities, and practice and play time comparable to those found on the men's soccer team.

People who argue that girls and women are not interested in athletics are embracing another fallacy. The Women's Sports Foundation reports that, in 1971, less than 1 percent of high school girls took part in interscholastic athletics. That figure rose to 26.7 percent of high school girls in the 1977–1978 school year, the compliance deadline for Title IX, and to 30.5 percent in 1990–1991. In 1993, 37 percent of high school athletes and 31 percent of NCAA Division I athletes were female.[8] A 1991 National Sporting Goods Association survey of 10,000 households found that 28 percent of women are frequent participants in the seven leading fitness activities, compared to 23 percent of men.[9]

Despite such progress, the struggle continues.

Basketball Hall of Fame member Carol Blazejowski commented, "It was a bigger struggle for me as a woman in a man's game." That's a large part of the problem that contributes to men's difficulty in accepting women in competitive sports. Men, historically, have created the games that we play. Nelson Doubleday was the creator of baseball. Dr. James Naismith was the first to perch a peach basket on top of a pole, thus originating the game of basketball. The list goes on. This creates an inherent feeling deep in the male soul that women can't possibly grasp the concepts, techniques, emotions, and methods of sports.

Men who adhere to that notion have never watched Chris Evert dispatch an opponent with cool steel on the red clay at the French Open, have never admired a supremely conditioned Martina Navratilova totally dominate hapless opponents on the lawn at Wimbledon. Indeed, some of the greatest achievements in sports belong to women: Bonnie Blair, Jackie Joyner-Kersee, Martina Navratilova, Nancy Lopez, and Ann Meyers.

Athletics is neither a sociological nor an academic pursuit, yet it is part of both. Sports is a significant part of American society. Some ask why a large portion of the population places such great emphasis on competitive athletics. The question should be, what is good about athletics? Is there value in athletics?

Athletics is part of a universal fabric. It is revered, scrutinized, analyzed, but always cherished. The media devote space and airtime to it, and corporations pour billions of dollars into sponsorship, advertising, and endorsements. For young people, athletics can teach teamwork, sportsmanship, poise in handling adversity, and discipline. It can also provide self-esteem through achievement and physical fitness. At any level, one of the most important lessons is that no reward is achieved without sacrifice.

These values are important for everyone. The percentage of athletes that advance from high school to a college scholarship is minuscule, and those that progress from a college scholarship to a sports professional's paycheck are even fewer. The gifted usually advance to their proper place. But for those who don't run fast enough, jump high enough, or throw far enough, the life lessons learned through athletics will be needed.

Sports is a microcosm of society in that many, if not all, of the attributes required to compete and be successful in the athletic arena are prerequisites for basic survival. Whether it is in business, law, or medicine, people need the skills to work as a team, to be able to function effectively under pressure, and to exhibit simpler traits like responsibility and discipline. Are these characteristics not as important for our daughters to learn as they are for our sons?

In the 1993 "Miller Lite Report on Sports and Fitness in the Lives of Working Women," between 36 percent and 41 percent of the women surveyed felt that involvement in sports and exercise helps them in the workplace. More specifically, 41 percent of women executives and 43 percent of women middle managers agree that sports and fitness activities help them "tap into the business network." Additionally, women executives (41 percent) agree that sports and fitness activities have advanced their career.[10]

Tennis Hall-of-Famer Billie Jean King recalled her historic match with infamous chauvinist Bobby Riggs in 1973. "I felt like I was representing people who believed in women's sports. I wanted to reinforce the fact that women and girls deserve the same opportunities to play at all levels. The public and the media always thought women would fold in the clutch. I just listened to the broadcast last year [1992] for the first time. As I listened to it, everybody thought I would fold because of my gender. You don't fold because of your gender, you fold because of your training. And women are trained differently [than men]."

This is the dilemma facing women in athletics. Men, money, and the media control modern-day sports. The organizations that represent teams and athletes do not necessarily look out for the best interests of the individuals involved. The goal is to present the product that will generate the greatest revenue.

This quest for the proverbial brass ring has been the primary justification offered for perpetuating the disparity between men and women in athletics. Historically, two men's sports have been the sources of revenue in collegiate athletics. Football and basketball have generated large sums of money over the years. With the emergence of "March Madness" more than a decade ago and the increase in payouts for football bowl games, these two sports have become the foundations from which institutions have claimed to support an entire athletic infrastructure.

Revenue is not prevalent in women's athletics, and only one, women's basketball, has emerged as a potential moneymaker. The prevailing thought process has awarded men's basketball and football larger slices of the budget pie in order for those teams to continue to compete for the pot of gold that is keeping the rest of the athletic department financially solvent.

Recent statistics, however, undress this theory as a monstrous fallacy. According to the NCAA's own statistics, only one-fifth of all NCAA athletic departments operate in the black. Bottom lines are not balancing out, as the old boys' network would lead one to believe.

These inconsistencies carry over to the premier professional sports for women: golf and tennis. A simple comparison of purses awarded shows that men in the middle (or lower) portion of their rankings consistently earn as much or more than the elite women in the same sport. Much of this is directly tied to sponsorship money as well as television revenue. While networks are making a conscious effort to schedule more women's events, sponsorship dollars and endorsement opportunities for women lag woefully behind.

Perhaps no other sports industry displays the inequity with such startling reality as much as women in the sports media. An analysis of the top daily newspapers in the United States shows that there are fewer than ten women sports editors nationwide. Additionally, the electronic media appear to have a quota system for women. It is unwritten and positively denied, but each of the networks has one woman, possibly two, but usually no more than two. Quite frequently those two don't have particularly glamorous or demanding responsibilities. For many years, television executives have justified these hiring practices with this simple axiom: "Most televised sports are watched by a primarily male audience. My advertisers are trying to reach this male audience. Males know everything there is to know about sports. Female sportscasters can't possibly explain a free safety blitz to Joe Six-pack." The Phyllis George/Jayne Kennedy syndrome didn't help either. All looks, no substance.

In youth and high school athletics, the battle often centers around resources, or the lack of them. Boys' teams traditionally have had newer uniforms, better equipment, preferred practice and game times, and more luxurious travel accommodations. While the boys' team travels to its game on the Greyhound bus, the girls' team is crammed into two school vans, with all of their equipment, to make the same trek. This system was, and sometimes still is, unwisely rationalized by stating that girls aren't particularly interested in competitive athletics. A decade ago, studies would show this argument to be true. What those studies did not show was that not enough opportunities were being offered to the girls to participate. If the administrators had thought to provide girls with the opportunity to play soccer, lacrosse, volleyball, golf, or track and field, participation numbers might have reflected a greater interest. That excuse no longer exists.

According to the Women's Sports Foundation and the National Sporting Goods Association:

- More than 8.2 million American girls and women play basketball
- 3.8 million girls and women play soccer
- 8.5 million girls and women run or jog.[11]

Why do men protest so much? Is it perceived that women are taking something away from men if they break the sports barrier? Will the last bastion of male bonding and privacy be lost? Perhaps men fear that including and accepting women in athletics will cause them to lose the last domain of male exclusivity. After all, women have made so much progress in all other facets of society. If a guy can't go down to Joe's Bar & Grill and watch the game on the big-screen television, have a cold beer, ogle the cheerleaders, and socialize with the guys, what will the world come to?

Maybe men feel that the acceptance of women in athletics would be sacrilegious—the equivalent of desecrating the legends of Jim Thorpe, the Gas House Gang, Murderers' Row, the Fearsome Foursome, Dick Butkus, the Steel Curtain, Vince Lombardi, and Knute Rockne all in one fell swoop. Sports would be emasculated forever. Experts suggest that these reasons are ancient, that they haven't heard them in years. Perhaps the feelings remain, but are better understood.

Jackson Katz is project director of the Mentors in Violence Prevention (MVP) Project at the Center for the Study of Sport in Society at Northeastern University in Boston, Massachusetts. Katz specializes in the social construction of masculinity through sports and media imagery. According to Katz,

> This relates to the construction of masculinity. It's very similar to why men are threatened [by women] in the military, and in occupations such as firemen, policemen and the construction trades. If you read the popular debate about women in those fields, people will say things like, there are a limited number of jobs and they want to hold onto their jobs. If you open it up to women through federal mandates to allow women, there will be less jobs for men. This misses a very big piece of the puzzle. This type of work brings satisfaction, not only for financial reasons, but because it is men doing manly jobs. The construction worker is the archetypal man, he lifts stones, builds buildings . . . manly things. If a woman can do the job, the status of the job becomes devalued. If a woman can do it, it must not be manly.
>
> The resistance to women in these jobs, is not out of fear that the women can't succeed. It's out of fear that the woman *can* do the job, thus reducing the status of men doing the job. Men are scrambling to keep women out of combat [in the military]. The ideological core of the military is combat, and the ideological mission of the military is about masculinity. In the modern era, with high-tech weapons, the nature of the battlefield has changed. It is no longer the soldier marching into battle. Strength is a weak argument . . . the argument that women don't have the upper body strength. Women can push a button as well as a man. What all of that hides is that the military markets itself to men, this is where you can come and prove you are a real man. The military takes boys and makes men. If a woman can do it, it mustn't be so manly. The moment you allow women to succeed in combat, it no longer is attractive to men.

Is it the simple resistance to change? A natural feeling. But isn't change good? If men feel threatened, there is some justification for that impression.

Within the last two years, women have not only progressed in women's athletics, but have ventured into men's athletics as well. Manon Rheaume made professional sports history in 1993 when she was the goaltender for the Tampa Bay Lightning in a hockey exhibition game and for two regular season games for Atlanta of the International Hockey League. Erin Whitten followed in Rheaume's footsteps in 1994 by minding the net for the Adirondack Red Wings of the American Hockey League.

Ila Borders became the first woman to pitch in an NCAA or NAIA baseball game when she started and went the distance for Southern California College in a 12–1 victory over Claremont-Mudd in 1994. Borders gave up just five hits, walked three, and struck out two. Two other women had played in collegiate baseball games before, but none had pitched. Borders had a solid season for Southern California College and has aspirations of playing in the big leagues. At Whittier Christian High School, Borders collected a 16–7 record in four seasons, with an ERA of 2.37, 165 strikeouts in 147 innings, team most valuable player recognition, and first team all-league nomination.[12]

In the 1992 Winter Olympics, the United States won eleven medals, but all five U.S. gold medals were won by women.[13] Susan O'Malley is not only a Jeopardy clue, but she is also president of the Washington Bullets of the National Basketball Association. She is the top-ranking female in professional sports, excluding women involved in ownership. Despite the fact that the Bullets' winning percentage has declined each year since 1988, O'Malley's first as executive vice president, the Bullets' attendance and season ticket sales have continued to rise. She was named president in 1991, and she oversees all off-court activity including television deals, promotions, and advertising campaigns.[14]

"Sports isn't an arena unto itself," Katz said. "Sports is one place where gender politics is right on the front burner. If women can succeed in sports that are traditionally men's sports, it is no longer masculine."

The two most threatening events pointed to by staunch male supporters are the recent emergence of the America3 all-women's crew in the America's Cup yacht racing series in 1995, and the formation of the Colorado Silver Bullets baseball team in 1993, an all-female baseball team with the objective of competing against men.

Experts will agree that neither group presents a serious threat to their male counterparts; however, the competition aspect is not really the ominous item. In both cases, the more foreboding aspect is that substantial money backed the ventures. Bill Koch, president of the America3 syndicate, vowed that *Mighty Mary* would be the first all-female boat to race in the 144-year history of the America's Cup.

He backed that up with substantial resources, and then an encouraging set of events elevated the status of *Mighty Mary*. The team acquired more than $10 million worth of corporate sponsorship: Chevrolet with a donation of $2.5 million; Yoplait yogurt, $2 million; L'Oreal, $1.5 million; and seven corporations at $750,000 apiece. Merchandisers also jumped aboard when the crew had its own candy bar, coffee, and wine.[15] The historic team of twenty-eight women (and one man, Dave Dellenbaugh) was not only competitive in the water, but sank the competition in the area usually dominated by men. Consider the fact that these *Fortune* 500 corporations that climbed aboard are probably directed by men, from their CEOs to their boards and top executives.

For Koch to convince those people, and then for those people to respond in a positive fashion speaks volumes. Think about it. Male-dominated *Fortune* 500 companies spent millions of the corporations' dollars to sponsor an all-female boat in the most prestigious sailing event in the world. What if the all-female team bombed out, wouldn't it be embarrassing for the corporate sponsors? How do you explain that to the board of directors? But marketing executives and advertisers utilized sound judgment. Some basic marketing dynamics were at work. Unique, historical, and unusual are three axioms marketers can't always find.

Perhaps as alarming to male sports fans is the development of the Silver Bullets. This team advanced the America3 concept. Both teams have all-female teams competing against men; both teams have substantial corporate sponsorship. What the Silver Bullets have that America3 didn't, though, is former major-league players coaching and managing the team.

The Coors Brewing Company underwrote the team's initial $3 million operating budget, and former Atlanta Braves' pitcher Phil Niekro was hired to manage the club, and he was joined by former major league pitcher and brother, Joe, as pitching coach (what else) and former Baltimore Orioles' outfielder Paul Blair. The team president, Bob Hope (no, not that Bob Hope) is also a former major league team executive. Organized baseball formally banned women from the minor leagues in 1953, but the Silver Bullets were officially admitted as an affiliate member of the independent Northern League by the National Association of Professional Baseball Leagues.[16]

The Silver Bullets' inaugural fifty-game schedule against minor league and collegiate teams was not a statistical success, and Hall-of-Famer Ted Williams's contention that the hardest feat to accomplish in any professional sport is to hit a baseball certainly proved true. America3 did not perform much better and certainly didn't panic Dennis Conner's Stars & Stripes or

PACT95's Young America. Many proponents of women's athletics derided the efforts of both of these squads as nothing more than novelty. If the argument is whether these all-female teams can ever be successful against male competition, the advocates for women's athletics have a point. But the true significance of these two efforts is that men and money unconditionally supported these two teams.

"One way to look at this is that society has taught young boys for centuries that to be female is to be second class," Katz stated. "We've all had coaches who said things like, 'you throw like a girl,' or 'you play like a bunch of sissies.' My identity as a man was on the line with Bobby Riggs [against Billie Jean King]. When I was in sixth grade, the fastest girl challenged me, the fastest boy, to a foot race. If I lost that race, I would have been humiliated."

In her latest book, *The Stronger Women Get, the More Men Love Football: Sexism and the American Culture of Sports*, author Mariah Burton Nelson echoes Katz's sentiments. In a newspaper interview about her book, Nelson said, "Little boys are still told 'You throw like a girl,' as an insult. Or parents will tell their own daughters, 'You throw like a boy,' and mean it as a compliment." Nelson continued, in the article, to explain that the use by athletes and coaches of vulgar epithets that denigrate women or women's bodies is "extremely prevalent, as kids get older." Boys in high school or college report that their coaches consistently use derogatory female terms as a way to motivate them.

Nelson noted, "These boys learn an extremely negative association with women's bodies. They learn to associate athleticism, toughness, and dominance with masculinity, so when that boy who has been ridiculed as feminine goes into a loving, romantic relationship with a girl, there's no way he can actually see her as a peer because his whole sense of self, of masculinity, has been defined as superior to women."[17]

The fact remains that men possess the lion's share of control in athletics, worldwide and in all aspects: coaching, administration, participation, media, and so on. What steps can be taken to enable women to crash the old boys' network? There are many proposals and suggestions to remedy these attitudes, but it must start on another level in a different manner.

2

Calling All Dads

Women are always nervous about being aggressive. Parents don't even realize this. And it's not done on purpose. But girls are taught to be passive from the pink blanket to when she falls down, to how they are held, how they are talked to, how they are told they are pretty. If a boy falls down, the father says, "Get up, you're okay." If a girl falls down, they say, "Oh, are you all right?" She's being told to be passive. If a woman is aggressive, people say she's a bitch, they don't like it. But women and men need to be appropriately aggressive. And we're not.

—Hall of Fame tennis player
Billie Jean King

Unfortunately for Sarah Manning, she is far removed from the protection and rights granted by Title IX. In the spring of 1995, Manning wanted to do nothing more than play baseball. As a fourteen-year-old high school freshman, Manning failed to make the varsity softball team at Kennard-Dale in York County, Pennsylvania, and she thought a year in the all-boys' baseball league would sharpen her skills for softball tryouts the following spring. The Delta Area Baseball and Softball for Youth League sent Manning to the bench without an at-bat.

Through 1991 the league permitted girls to play baseball with boys in the Delta Area organization. Manning and her two sisters, Shannon and

Bryana, all played baseball prior to the league's decision following the 1991 season.[1] The league claims its decision was to bolster a floundering softball league that had only two teams and minimal participation. According to one league official, however, the softball league was doing fine in 1995, and she was not sure what was behind the prohibition of Sarah Manning.[2]

Manning, who played first base and catcher for the Delta Hornets softball team in 1994, batted .559 with nineteen hits, including four doubles and ten runs batted in.[3] For no legitimate reasons, Manning will not be able to make the transition to the baseball diamond. Is it sexism? Discrimination?

Manning and her parents were given a variety of reasons why Sarah could not play baseball in the summer of 1995—concerns about competitiveness and safety, as well as fairness because of a rule that prohibits boys from playing softball. Ironically, Fawn Grove, a neighboring town with a league identical to Delta, allows girls to play baseball. Both leagues are affiliated with the Mason-Dixon Baseball and Softball for Youth League. According to Martin Pomraning, Mason-Dixon president, the organization has no policy distinguishing which sports girls can and cannot play. Pomraning believes Manning should be allowed to play.[4]

The Mason-Dixon association is an umbrella organization that sets standards for game rules and basic organizational strategies; however, each of the five affiliates has its own board of directors with separate bylaws. The Delta Area bylaws, dated 1985, do not prohibit girls from playing any sports.[5]

A male Delta board member said that the girls were being excluded for safety concerns and stated, matter of factly, that Manning would get hurt. Another Delta board member made the preposterous proclamation that they would not want to see girls get hurt and that the boys are supposed to be tough enough to take it. It was also suggested that Sarah could go to Fawn Grove if she wanted to play baseball.[6]

The Delta league vice president was questioned by a newspaper reporter as to whether Sarah and other girls would be competitive with the boys. The league official responded that Sarah and other girls in her age group would not be competitive at that level.[7] The question of competitiveness is not an issue. If the boys who play in the league are not denied a roster spot because of their ability, or lack of it, neither should Manning. The issue is the opportunity to participate, and Manning has been denied that opportunity.

When Manning's mother, Elizabeth, tried to register her daughter for baseball in January 1995, she was told her daughter could not play with the boys. When she protested, no action was taken. Her check was not cashed, but she did force the board of directors to vote.

After the league's initial stance taken in early April, when the story first appeared in the newspapers, the league board of directors apparently changed their minds—at least on the reasons behind the ban. Originally, the board had cited safety, fairness, and competitiveness as its primary concerns. When the media spotlight forced the board to vote, in mid-April, the board again voted "no." The board president stated a February decision to let Sarah play was rescinded when Sarah and her mother rejected her team assignment. The league stated that it was not a matter that Sarah wanted to play baseball but that the Mannings also wanted to determine the team on which she would play. The board president also intimated that, when the story received media attention, it demeaned the program, another factor in the decision to ban Sarah.[8]

Manning's parents had hoped for a public discussion and an open vote on the topic, but instead the board made the announcement of its unanimous decision without any input from outside sources. The statement said the existing policy, developed in 1991, would stand. This is a policy that is not in the league's bylaws. The board said it would take any questions on the matter at its November meeting[9]—after Sarah Manning's summer had been ruined.

Equally irritating for the gatekeepers of the all-boys' club was the Little League World Series of 1993. Much to the chagrin of Little League Baseball, Inc., as well as many of its supporters, Kathy Barnard became the first woman to coach a team to the Little League World Series. Barnard guided her son's North Vancouver British Columbia Little League team to the Williamsport, Pennsylvania extravaganza. Barnard acknowledged that her experience was one few mothers would have, and she deemed it a "memory of a lifetime." When she isn't coaching, Barnard is playing third base, shortstop, and left field in three softball leagues. But Barnard, along with her two brothers, earned her training on the diamond playing Little League baseball.[10]

The same can't be said of girls in 1995. Although Congress rewrote Little League Baseball's federal charter in 1973 to enable girls to play, the international headquarters in Williamsport still vaguely recognizes girls' participation. When questioned about the number of girls who play Little League baseball, the director of communications, Dennis M. Sullivan, wrote that he was unable to supply that information because Little League doesn't keep records of the race, creed, or gender of its participants.

Ironically, the organization was able to confirm that Barnard was the first female to coach a team in the Little League World Series, and Sullivan confirmed that there are approximately 300,000 participants in Little League Softball programs around the world.

Grudgingly, Little League Baseball, Inc., must be given credit. When the federal government intervened more than twenty years ago so that girls could play Little League, the organization quietly frowned on that decision. Little League took the "Citadel approach." In 1995 a variety of courts ruled that Shannon Faulkner had to be admitted to that state-run, all-male military institution unless the Citadel could develop a comparable alternate program at a sister institution. Little League Baseball decided to develop Little League Softball.

Little League Baseball, Inc., is arguably the largest, most well-known youth sports program in the world today: 2.7 million players on 180,000 teams in 77 countries, with 1 million volunteers. The commitment to softball by the Williamsport-based organization has given young girls something most other youth leagues have not—an opportunity to participate.

According to Little League literature, Little League Softball, which was inaugurated in 1974, is designed for girls from nine to twelve years of age. It has approximately 3,500 chartered programs. It also includes a T-ball league for girls from six to eight years old and Minor League programs for less formal instruction. Little League Softball also features a full range of tournament play, including the Little League Softball World Series held in Kalamazoo, Michigan.

Little League must also be given credit for vision and development. Senior League Softball, designed for girls from thirteen to fifteen years old, currently has more than 1,850 chartered programs. Based on the popularity of its first two leagues, the organization rolled out Big League Softball in 1980, targeted at sixteen- to eighteen-year-olds. This division claims 520 chartered programs.

Thankfully for Felicia Finley, she didn't belong to either of the aforementioned organizations. In the summer of 1995, Finley became the first girl to ever play in the Wren Youth Association Coaches Pitch all-star game. At four feet tall and sixty-five pounds, Finley may not have looked like most of her counterparts, but she played as well or better than most of them. During the four-game, round robin series against other Anderson County, South Carolina, all-star teams, Finley went 5-for-9 at the plate.

Finley's all-star coach, Steve Campbell, described her as a "natural" and confirmed there was never a question whether Finley would make the team. Campbell cited Finley's hustle, hitting, strong arm, and knowledge of the game as her strongest attributes. The third-grader-to-be was rated ninth out of 160 candidates for the all-star team. Finley was not the only girl to play in this league. According to league officials, approximately twenty girls participated in the summer of 1995.

Although Finley faced some resistance in her attempt to play in the Wren league, and despite her parent's apprehension, Finley wants to progress to Little League next summer. While Little League is more competitive than the Wren league, Campbell feels that Finley will be able to adjust, if she wants to. Her parents indicated they will let Felicia make that decision when the time comes.[11]

The predicament for girls in the elementary school age group is that the majority of youth athletic programs at this level are run by community organizations which rely on volunteers for coaching and administration. Funding for these organizations is also voluntary; leagues host a myriad of bake sales, bumper sticker drives, and candy bar blitzes. Entrance fees also count, so attracting interest is paramount. Most, if not all, of these programs are not subject to the federal law, Title IX. Probably none of these programs receive federal funding for their operation. In the case of Sarah Manning, there was consideration for legal action against the municipality for discriminatory use of its athletic fields, but it is doubtful such action would be subject to federal, or even state, enforcement.

There are two dilemmas for girls and parents of this age group. Opportunities are not readily available, because of some of the aforementioned factors, and parents, specifically fathers, do not actively encourage their daughters to participate in athletics. This is not, necessarily, a conscious omission, but one that is a product of society. Daughters do not have the same openings in youth leagues their fathers had.

In 1985 Miller Lite and the Women's Sports Foundation conducted a poll and published a report called the "Miller Lite Report on Women in Sports." One of the questions asked was, "In your opinion, which of the following are the biggest barriers to increased participation by women in sports and fitness?" The random sample of more than 7,000 respondents claimed, as their number one answer, "Lack of involvement and training as children (45 percent)." This same poll showed that 31 percent of the respondents did not participate on pre–high school athletic teams.[12]

"The Wilson Report: Moms, Dads, Daughters and Sports" (1988) corroborated the Miller Lite findings. In a random telephone survey of more than 1,000 mothers and fathers, and 513 of their seven- to eighteen-year-old daughters, only 35 percent of daughters seven to ten years of age and 28 percent of daughters eleven to fourteen years of age became involved in athletics through community organizations; 24 percent of seven- to ten-year-olds and 18 percent of eleven- to fourteen-year-olds become involved through private organizations; and just 6 percent of seven- to ten-year-olds and 11 percent of eleven- to fourteen-year-olds participated through their church organization.[13] More recent statistics show an increase; however, it is still insufficient. According to the 1993 "Miller Lite Report on Sports and Fitness in the Lives of Working Women," prior to the passage of Title IX in 1972, only 48 percent of all girls participated in youth sports; 64 percent took part after the passage of the law.[14]

Donna Lopiano, the executive director of the Women's Sports Foundation, recognizes the difficulties faced by parents and daughters in youth league situations. "The youth sports situation is much more complicated because youth sports has traditionally been a community volunteer function at the lowest levels," Lopiano explained. "It has been rotary clubs, it has been parks and recreation commissions, it has been all those parents who have to run the show for youth sports. And what's happened is that as parks and recreation program funds have dried up, kids who are not looking at sport as an alternative are choosing negative alternatives. We have got to realize the stakes in terms of what we are going to pay for in crimes and teenage pregnancies. There needs to be a national movement to really bring public attention to the importance of after-school activities for kids during this high risk period of time."

The responsibility for these programs and for the development of daughters' athletic skills falls squarely on the shoulders of parents. According to the Wilson report, the two largest deterrents for girls in youth sports is lack of skills (49 percent) and lack of opportunities (30 percent).[15] How many men grew up playing catch in the backyard or shooting baskets in the driveway with their fathers? How many women can make the same claim?

It probably hasn't been a very masculine thing, according to society, for a father to come home from work and ask his daughter if she wants to throw the ball around after supper. It's more appropriate, most assume, to play with the doll house (which most dads won't participate in, either) or read a story. But while evidence supports the contention that attitudes have changed in this regard, behavior has not followed the same course.

The Wilson report indicated that 87 percent of today's moms and dads generally accept the idea that sports are equally important for boys and girls. Parents also show very little concern that sports may be un-ladylike, and nearly all agree (97 percent) that sports and fitness activities provide important benefits to girls who participate. Parents' own behavior also influences their daughters, since parents who play tend to have daughters who play—70 percent of the daughters who currently participate have parents who also engage in sports and fitness activities.[16]

More than any other advantage, parents value a daughter's sports experience because it contributes to her physical well-being; when asked how girls benefit from sports, 55 percent of parents mentioned physical and health factors. Sports and fitness activities also build confidence and self-esteem (41 percent); they promote teamwork, foster cooperation, and encourage friendships (27 percent).[17] Furthermore, 33 percent of the parents of the girls who currently participate in sports and fitness activities wish their daughters were more involved in athletics, and 63 percent of parents of daughters who quit playing wish they had continued.[18]

All that having been said, the following statistic, then, is the most startling. Of all the seven- to ten-year-olds surveyed, only 27 percent of those girls say their father is the one who most encourages them to play sports.[19] Twenty-seven percent! Why is that?—especially considering the importance of this encouragement to little girls, with 44 percent of all daughters surveyed emphasizing that their parents' participation in their sports activities is the encouragement they remember the most. It is time for fathers to step up to the plate or the free throw line and execute an important play.

"Right now, the [youth] situation is being policed by fathers who are angry," according to Lopiano. "You are the first generation of fathers who have come through the sixties and seventies and grown up believing that your daughters will have equal opportunity. You will really be teed off to find out that she doesn't. Especially if she happens to like soccer, or other sports that are not sponsored. You will really be teed off to find out that just because someone else has two sons and you have two daughters, the sons' teams are sponsored. . . . I think the big difference has been DADS who are bringing pressure to bear."

Fathers and mothers can get assistance from a variety of sources, and Lopiano's organization is a good place to start. The Women's Sports Foundation (WSF), established in 1974 by founder Billie Jean King, was joined by other champion athletes of the day, including swimmer Donna de Varona, Micki King Hogue, Wyomia Tyus, and Sheila Young Ochowitz. It is a nonprofit, educational organization that serves as a collective voice and national network for those who are dedicated to promoting and enhancing the sports experience for all girls and women. The foundation provides programs and services in the areas of education, opportunity, recognition, and advocacy:

1. Education—the foundation works to improve public understanding of the benefits of sports and fitness for females of all ages. It has a resource center, a library, and an 800 number to answer most questions about women's sports. Materials include sports guides and brochures, videos, and research reports.

2. Opportunity—the foundation provides direct grants or empowers others to provide opportunities for girls and women in sports through the Travel and Training Fund, the Leadership Development Fund, the Coaches Advisory Roundtable (CAR), internships, and grassroots grants programs.

3. Recognition—foundation programs recognize the achievements of girls and women in sports as participants, leaders, and role models.

4. Advocacy—the foundation works to promote legislation and policies in government and within sports organizations that would increase the number and quality of opportunities for girls and women in sports. The foundation works with sports governing groups, governmental agencies, legislators, and other women's sports advocates to promote sports opportunities for girls and women.

One of the areas in which the WSF concentrates is increasing funding and interest in sports programs for girls. In 1991 the WSF and Tampax Tampons launched the Tampax Grants for Girls program. The program distributed 100 $1,000 grants to sports programs serving girls from nine to fourteen years old. It was an attempt to address the problem of girls dropping out of sports at this age and to provide the experience they need to play sports in high school. Additionally, in 1987, the WSF created the first annual National Girls and Women in Sports Day.

"The Women's Sports Foundation is really a sleeping giant that had been in existence for twenty years," Lopiano said. "It was established by Billie Jean King and Donna de Varona and a lot of other champion athletes of their day who were committed to not having little girls follow in their footsteps—facing the same barriers that they did. The foundation is the only organization that has an umbrella interest in sports. It cares about all women's sports—all age levels. We have a very broad interest. We have access to highly visible champion athletes who speak on the cause and who instantly get good press. As far as being a voice for women's sports, the foundation has been in a very unique position to play that role."

Another of the five organizations that coordinate National Girls and Women in Sports Day is the National Association for Girls and Women in Sport (NAGWS). This is an association of the American Alliance for Health, Physical Education, Recreation, and Dance. It is a nonprofit, educational organization designed to serve the needs of administrators, teachers, coaches, leaders, and participants of sports programs for girls and women. One of six associations of the alliance, the NAGWS is the only national professional organization devoted exclusively to providing opportunities for girls and women in sport-related disciplines and careers.

Among the goals and objectives of the NAGWS is developing quality sports programs designed to accommodate females of all ages, races, creeds, ethnic origins, economic levels, abilities, and interests. To that end, the NAGWS plays a big part in National Girls and Women in Sports Day, held annually each February. The NAGWS oversees production and distribution of the Community Action Kit and serves as the contact for all state coordinators of the event.

Advocacy, foundations, associations, high-profile athletes championing the cause—seems like the gender equity struggle is moving in the right direction. Or is it?

Lake Superior College Library

3

Varsity Jackets and Letter Sweaters

Those in education have a role to play. It is one thing to have a passion for sports and it is entirely another thing to leap to an expectation of public support without the critical educational piece. One of the things we have been trying to do is point out to parents that every time we cut a team, every time we cut band, every time we cut an afterschool activity—we are putting one more kid on the streets. We know girls who play sports are 80 percent less likely to be involved in unwanted pregnancies and 92 percent less likely to be involved in drugs—and three times more likely to graduate from high school. We know all of these things. We just have to let the taxpayer be aware of what the stakes are when we take sports opportunities away from our kids or we don't give them to our daughters.
—Donna Lopiano, Executive Director,
Women's Sports Foundation

The folks in western Nebraska haven't got it yet, at least according to parents and female student-athletes in the Fremont, Holdrege, Minden, and North Platte school districts. In April 1995, student-parent groups brought federal lawsuits against these school districts for alleged Title IX violations. Each of those districts operates one high school, and the suits filed in the U.S. District Court in Omaha maintained that these school districts failed to provide their female students with equal opportunities to participate in interscholastic sports.

More specifically, the lawsuits charged that, compared to the boys' programs, the girls received inferior sports equipment, supplies, and uniforms and unequal scheduling, travel, per diems, coaching, locker rooms, cheerleading, band performances, and publicity. The complaints wanted softball to be added to the sports offerings for girls in these school districts and for these female athletes to be treated equitably. One parent claimed the district argued that girls aren't as interested in sports as boys.

School officials claimed cost was a problem for adding softball, and that softball was new to Nebraska high schools, so competition, or the lack of it, was also a concern. Varsity softball for girls was introduced to Nebraska high schools in 1993, and only 30 of the 345 high schools in the Nebraska School Activities Association offer the sport. They are primarily Class A schools in the state's two metropolitan areas of Lincoln and Omaha. In Nebraska, state championships are offered in eleven boys sports and ten girls sports.[1]

The parents of the girls in the lawsuits felt that adding softball would balance the inequities in the athletics programs, and they even went as far as to organize a private group to develop and fund a network of club softball teams. The intent was to demonstrate the interest level in softball. Parents of a student at Minden dished out $3,500 to help sponsor their daughter's team. In the fall of 1994, there were a combined thirty-seven girls in the junior and senior high school at Minden involved in the club softball program, but the district would not change its mind on offering softball as a varsity sport.[2]

Additionally, one parent contended that girls' basketball games were played in midweek, while boys played on weekends. This particular parent stated that her daughter was pulled from a class at 2:00 P.M., traveled two hours by bus to the game, played the game, and returned home at 1:00 A.M. and then started to study for three tests she had scheduled on the following day.[3]

The superintendent of Holdrege schools, D. Dale Deriese, explained that offering softball as a varsity sport would be a disadvantage to the girls because the girls would have to choose between cross country, volleyball, golf, and softball. He asserts that as long as softball remained a club sport, the girls can play more than one sport.[4] What?

In mid-August 1995, the Holdrege district settled a class-action suit by committing to add girls' varsity fast-pitch softball in the fall of 1995. The settlement committed Holdrege to continuing softball as a varsity sport for at least four years. It also required the school to promote the sport.[5]

Cross country and golf, especially at the high school level, do not lend themselves to large participation numbers. Volleyball is the second most popular sport among girls and young women, and it welcomes a substantial number of participants. Offering softball makes a great deal of sense from a participation standpoint, and interest has been demonstrated, although, according to the law, it is not necessarily a prerequisite for the district to offer the sport.

"The first thing I would ask the school, is have you done an interest survey," said Susan True. "Because our tendency is to think in terms of interest in sports as it relates to boys. But there is also fencing, swimming, synchronized swimming, tennis, golf, etc. Schools that have done interest surveys are really surprised at how many girls are interested in sports they are not offering. Schools don't want to be told that in order to comply they will probably have to offer more sports for girls than for boys. Quite frankly, schools need to find out if they are offering what they ought to be offering."

True is an assistant director at the National Federation of State High School Associations, and she has been with the organization for thirteen years. The role of the federation is to provide services to its member state high school associations. It was organized in 1920 to try to bring some consistency and appropriateness to the rules governing high school competition in athletics. Unfortunately, as a service organization, it has no enforcement power.

"We know, for instance, that the high school level is about the same as the college level [statistically]. And I think that is going to be the next legal ballpark," said Donna Lopiano. "The parents are going to start to court there [at the high school level]. They [the parents] have been more successful at the high school level in getting school boards to be responsive because these are their neighbors. They are not untouchable. We get calls all the time from parents who ask, what can I do. The first piece of advice we give them is, 'who do you know on the school board, who do you know on the city council.' Tell them what to do and usually they can put together enough public pressure to really effect change in a very internal way, and it is good."

According to the National Federation of State High School Associations, 817,073 girls participated in interscholastic high school athletics nationwide in 1972–1973. That total had increased to 2,240,461 in 1994–1995.[6] However, according to "The Wilson Report: Moms, Dads, Daughters and Sports" (1988), 87 percent of seven- to ten-year-old girls and 84 percent of eleven- to fourteen-year-old girls are involved in sports, but that number drops to 75 percent of girls in high school. One of the leading reasons for

this decrease in participation, according to the study, is the lack of opportunity.[7]

Other forms of discrimination exist, some not as blatant as others. Even
in the mid-1990s, as the Nebraska case shows, ignorance prevails. "For a
number of years, of course, high schools knew they needed at least as many
sports for girls as they had for boys," said True. "It hasn't been, of course,
until recently that people have become more aware of the fact that the
interpretation of Title IX also relates to the percentage of girls and boys in
the school."

"The way you see Title IX violations on the high school level are more
subtle," True explained. "Such as how teams travel to games. The boys
might go on a chartered bus, while the girls go in a van and the coach has
to drive the van. I hear from people who have done some research and
they find if they go to a state championship, the boys stay two to a room,
while the girls stay four in a room."

"Some people might say, well . . . part of that is the size of the male
basketball players," True continued. "But we have tall female basketball
and volleyball players, and if all of the girls' teams are accommodated in a
different way, then there is something else involved. I also don't think all
high schools have solved the issue of facilities."

True knows of other examples of inequity. True, a member of the Wom-
en's Sports Foundation, was working with Donna Lopiano several years ago
on a program that was awarding grant money to high school athletic programs specifically to assist with gender equity progress. "We were evalu-
ating applications for these grants, and we were absolutely appalled to hear
some of the situations that existed," True recalled. "At one high school,
for instance, the boys' teams were receiving new uniforms every two years,
while the girls' teams hadn't had new uniforms in seven years. There were
girls' basketball teams that were practicing with plywood placed in a parking
lot because they were not allowed in the gymnasium. I don't know if people
realize that is all part of equity. And that also sends a negative message to
young girls as to the value of girls participating in sports."

The dilemma at the high school level is not restricted to participation
opportunities for girls and the variety of grievances claimed in the Nebraska
lawsuits. There is a haunting absence of women in decision-making roles
on the interscholastic athletic level as well.

Sandra E. Scott, Ph.D., the executive director of the New York State
Public High School Athletic Association, has conducted extensive studies
to analyze women specifically in decision-making roles. One of the pre-
dicaments for Scott and her colleagues nationwide is that the lack of women

in such roles as athletic director, assistant athletic director, superintendent, and head coach is "overshadowed by the dramatic increase in sports participation for girls." The Title IX battle has centered around participation opportunities, while women to coach and administrate these programs have nearly been forgotten. Women as administrators and coaches provide important role models for girls and young women, and that is a critical piece of the debate that is missing.

Dr. Scott presented her findings to the annual meeting of the National Federation of State High School Associations in Nashville, Tennessee, in July 1993. The historical context of her study shows some of the drastic shifts that have taken place. In 1974, twenty-nine state associations had an advisory group on girls' athletics. According to Dr. Scott's survey, only ten states had such advisory groups in 1992. Also in 1974, ten state associations (California, Kansas, Maryland, Michigan, New Hampshire, New Jersey, Pennsylvania, Idaho, Washington, D.C., and Delaware) had a female representative on their board of control. A year later, the National School Boards Association conducted a similar survey to find out that women, voting and nonvoting, represented just 5 percent of all persons serving on all governing boards.[8] A 1980 follow-up survey indicated that twenty-nine state associations had one or more female voting members on their governing boards. A total of 100 women represented 7 percent of all board members, reflecting a 2 percent increase over a five-year period.[9]

"I think the job market, right now, might be hurting the battle for equity," True indicated. "Women are very, very afraid to make waves and lose their jobs. Because, unlike when I started and schools were clamoring for teachers, that is not the case now. So, do you put your job on the line?"

Dr. Scott surveyed the field again in 1992 and found some progress. The number of voting representatives had increased to 13 percent, based on a total number of 129 women. Thirty-seven state associations indicated one or more women on their board as compared to twenty-nine states in 1980. Fifty percent of the membership of the New York board are women; California is second with 37 percent. Other states that had more than 20 percent female representation included Minnesota, 30 percent; Montana and Iowa, 28 percent; Connecticut and Utah, 25 percent; New Hampshire, 23 percent; and Maryland and Michigan, 21 percent.[10] Most of these women were principals and superintendents followed by school board members. But if most states are reflective of New York, this trend is at a dead end. According to the New York State Education Department, women represent just 8.5 percent of the superintendents and 1.8 percent of the secondary principals in New York.[11]

Encouraged by her information gathering, Dr. Scott noted, at the time, that "the most significant change to occur is that state associations are requiring a specific number of women on their boards or adopting provisions to ensure gender as well as minority representation. Eight state associations now require a specific number of women on their boards of control: Arkansas, California, Iowa, Kentucky, New Jersey, New York, Wisconsin, and Wyoming."[12] Also in this survey, Dr. Scott identified six states that included provisions for gender/minority representation: Kansas, Michigan, Minnesota, South Carolina, Texas, Washington, Indiana, and Wisconsin.

Dr. Scott's own state association has been an exemplary model. Since 1975, the New York board has comprised eleven men and eleven women. Noticing that the representatives of girls' athletics were becoming more and more male, the association amended its constitution in 1991 to state "one male representative and one female representative of athletics from each section."[13]

In addition to women serving on state association governing boards, women should have the opportunity to serve on state sports committees and other standing committees influencing scholastic athletics. Thirty-four states (who responded) identified 5,579 such positions, or 25.6 percent.[14]

The numbers of women in interscholastic coaching positions and athletic directorships and women athletic officials have also dwindled, and that trend does not appear to be reversing itself. In the early 1970s it was estimated that 85 percent of the athletic administrators of girls' sports were women. In 1990, 87 percent of the directors of girls' sports were men. The decline is also evident in coaching and officiating. In 1973 approximately 90 percent of the coaches of girls' sports were women. According to Dr. Scott's 1992 survey, that percentage has fallen to 31 percent. Only 9.6 percent of all officials registered with state associations are women. These data, supplied by thirty-six states, reflected a range from 25 percent to 1 percent, with twenty state associations reporting 10 percent or less.[15]

True believes some of the decline is due to a peculiar progression. "Until the growth of girls' programs at the high school level, walk-on coaches were not a necessity," True said. "Many women were assigned seven or eight sports. In reality, all they were were chaperons. One of the dilemmas that occurred because of Title IX and the tremendous growth of girls' teams was they didn't have enough women to coach those teams.

"When they really start *coaching* the team it took too much time (to coach seven or eight)," True continued. "So women resigned from five or six of those teams, and stayed on to coach one, two, maybe three sports. Then the athletic director had to look for coaches for those other five or six teams.

Two things happened. First, studies have shown there are more men in coaching who are teaching subjects other than physical education than there are women. So, when the athletic director needed nine girls' team coaches, he only had two female physical education instructors. When he looked to the faculty to find a coach, he was more likely to find a man.

"The second thing was, for example, the women's basketball coaching position became open. It was a much more attractive job than it was five years before. The assistant coach for men says to himself, 'Maybe I am going to sit here forever as an assistant coach and I really want to be a head coach.' So he takes the women's head coaching job since most schools like to hire from within. So I think when our percentages dropped, maybe it wasn't in bodies so much, but that one woman who used to be counted eight times is only being counted twice now."

Yet even in the 1990s, there remains ignorance that leads to a lack of knowledge that deters the most genuine efforts. And many unwittingly display the primitive ideology that once prevailed in this discussion. Upon surveying the state associations nationwide in 1991 to determine the number of women coaching girls' teams, one oblivious male athletic director responded to Dr. Scott in writing: "Come on, aren't we past this kind of stuff?"[16]

Male coaches of female teams on all levels have had this thought. It will be repeated. The dilemma of too many males coaching female teams has nothing to do with coaching ability. As Dr. Scott responded to this particular inquiry: "Our female athletes must see women as coaches, officials, and administrators to know there are opportunities after participation, to know it is appropriate and acceptable for women to demonstrate competence and to display self-assurance, and to know that women in the sport world can direct their own futures."[17]

Through Dr. Scott's efforts and the cooperation of others, the National Federation of High School Associations, in 1993, approved the formation of an Equity Committee. At the same time, the federation adopted a constitutional amendment to ensure female and minority representation on the federation's Executive Committee, its primary governing board, as well as on all appropriate committees. The Equity Committee will address a long list of issues such as women and minority representation on state associations, assist in identifying qualified gender and minority candidates to serve on appropriate committees, and ensure that concerns and issues related to gender and minority representation receive appropriate federation attention.[18]

Fortunately, and unfortunately, the establishment is not always as cooperative as the National Federation of State High School Associations was in accepting the formation of the Equity Committee. Sometimes those who vigilantly maintain the power structure need a subtle reminder, like a whack in the side of the head with a two-by-four. Fortunately the constituents have federal, state, and district courts where they can pursue fair treatment. Unfortunately the legal system is not the most desirable venue to remedy this dilemma. Also regrettable, the legal system is not always knowledgeable enough to make the correct decision, thus gender equity enforcement continues at a snail's pace. Remarkably, the U.S. District Court in Montana had the understanding and knowledge to formulate a settlement in what should be a landmark Title IX legal brief.

In 1982 Karyn and Donna Ridgeway and a host of plaintiffs filed suit against the Montana High School Association (MHSA). Rather than proceed to court, the two sides, with guidance and motivation from the U.S. District Court, reached a settlement agreement and avoided a lengthy, expensive court battle.

Also named in the suit as defendants were the Montana Office of Public Instruction (OPI) and its superintendent, the executive director of the Montana High School Association, the high school districts named, along with their respective chairperson. The high school districts were Missoula County, Whitehall District No. 2, and Columbia Falls No. 6.

According to the documentation, the plaintiffs alleged they were denied equal opportunity to participate in extracurricular high school athletics and were subjected to "invidious discrimination" in athletics and consequently were deprived of an opportunity to develop to their full educational potential in violation of state and federal law.

Such discrimination was alleged to exist in the number of sanctioned sports available; the seasons in which sports were available; the length of the sport season; the scheduling of practice and games; and facilities, equipment, coaching, transportation, school band and pep rallies, uniforms, and access to trainers.

Joanne Austin began working for the Montana High School Association in 1986, ironically the same week the Ridgeway suit went to court over the one unresolved issue of scheduling. In Montana, Michigan, and a few other states, girls' basketball is played in the fall and volleyball in the winter, contrary to most other states. Austin was hired as an administrative assistant/ equity officer. The MHSA governs an association of more than 181 members.

"We were in tough times around here for gender equity," Austin said. "Unfortunately it took us a lawsuit to get here, but the good thing is our conditions are much better. We have more participants, we have better facilities, we have better rotations of schedules. All of those things as a result of the Ridgeway agreement. We have made tremendous progress in the last decade."

Still, it hasn't been easy. Austin was hired in her position as equity officer because the U.S. District Court directed the MHSA to appoint a gender equity officer. It is an official position, and very few, if any, other high school associations in the country have, on staff, an official equity officer in their association.

Of course, the defendants denied liability for the claims. The defendants also had the brazenness to challenge the court's jurisdiction over the subject matter of the litigation and over their persons. Additionally, the defendants denied that federal law covered the subject of extracurricular high school athletics and denied that the state agency defendant had any responsibility over the subject of litigation.

The defendants' claims were a complete farce. Any administrator remotely aware of Title IX knows that this federal law pertains to all educational institutions that receive federal money for any purpose for their educational mission. Furthermore, if the defendants firmly believed their defense, they would not have negotiated and accepted the agreement because it is comprehensive and overwhelmingly favors the plaintiffs.

According to the court, the intentions of the settlement agreement were to advance the opportunities that female high school students have to participate in extracurricular athletic events relative to their male counterparts; to create, implement, and enforce minimum requirements for obtaining sex equity in athletics in Montana; and to make available established grievance procedures and forums and to permit students experiencing sex inequities to obtain nonjudicial relief, while retaining the availability of alternative redress through remedies extended by state and federal law.

The agreement set forth a number of standards under its "General Terms." These provisions dictated the future conduct of the parties, established minimum requirements for sex equity in athletics and implementation of a grievance procedure and sanctions, outlined a plan of implementation, determined reporting requirements, and named a neutral facilitator. The most significant factor in the minimum requirements was setting a compliance date. That left no indecisiveness possible for the defendants. Additionally, minimum standards were determined for statewide as well as individual school district activity.

Statewide, agencies would be accountable for the number of sanctioned sports offered, the length of athletic seasons, the continuity of athletic seasons and the elimination of overlapping seasons, tournament locations, press releases, MHSA coaching requirements, summer camp rules, and recruiting efforts by the MHSA and officials.

Minimum requirements for the school districts also covered an expansive list. Some hallmark decisions were advanced. In addressing the number of offered sports, the court determined, "A limitation of funds shall not be a justification for offering an unequal number of sports for males and females."

In its second point, with regard to coaching, a three-part heading specified that coaches would undergo an annual review by their district, thus ensuring that girls would receive the same quality of coaching as their male counterparts.

The minimum requirements for school districts addressed other topics, including coaching salaries; publicity; team support; scheduling and facilities; laundry facilities; recognition boards, halls of fame, and trophy cases; meals; overnight accommodations and out-of-state trips; uniforms, accessories, equipment, and supplies; booster clubs; transportation; access to an athletic trainer; officials; recruiting efforts by school districts; and sex equity policy, grievance procedures, and coordinator.

The agreement also specified grievance procedures and sanctions, for both state and local districts, and determined that future plaintiffs need not exhaust the OPI or MHSA grievance procedures before pursuing matters in a U.S. district or federal court. In effect, the court made a statement to the MHSA and local districts. If fair treatment was not granted, the court would be glad to discuss the matter. Finally, the agreement drafted plans for the OPI to provide technical assistance for local school district, state, and national activities.

"What the Ridgeway agreement did, it gave us a tool, an instrument with which we could implement gender equity," Austin explained. "It was more specific than was Title IX at the time, and so now we have both. And I believe we are unique because we have the enforcement authority, because the U.S. District Court gave it to us."

This agreement was momentous. It was comprehensive in addressing every facet of interscholastic athletics, and it held accountable the alleged offending parties by establishing requirements and determining compliance dates for those standards. The appointment of a neutral facilitator maintained the flow of the process and, finally, the settlement preserved the future rights of any discriminated party to pursue the fullest legal action necessary and available.

Austin's job remains challenging, but difficult at times. Investigating complaints is probably the most arduous task she performs. "I've done investigations and visitations and looked into complaints and just done some random on-sight visitations where the school administrators and coaches have basically gritted their teeth and let me in because they know I have the authority to be there . . . but they really don't want me there. Overall I am treated with respect and openness. I have more positive than negative experiences, but part of me is always prepared for that [negative encounter].

"I am not in the business of slapping administrators on the wrist and saying, 'You know, you shouldn't have done that,' " Austin went on. "Ideally I should be assisting schools in increasing their programs. I don't like to view my position as an enforcement position. We want to educate everyone so they can come into compliance on their own.

"We continue to enforce the Ridgeway agreement," Austin continued. "We do random, on-sight visitations and we try to keep an ongoing dialogue with the member schools. We try to take advantage of any opportunity where a large number of our membership is represented so that we can conduct workshops and provide information. So this is something that is ongoing and will continue."

Over the years, Minnesota has been a national player at the forefront of positive Title IX activity. Recently, the Minnesota State High School League (MSHSL) developed a "Gender Equity in Athletics Manual." With technical assistance from the Minnesota Department of Education, this guide is designed to assist Minnesota schools in conducting a self-review of gender equity in their athletic programs. The manual has also been shared with the National Federation, as a model, and with other state associations or school districts requesting the material.

One of the individuals responsible for advocating equity for Minnesota schools is Dorothy McIntyre. McIntyre is the associate executive director of the Minnesota High School League, and she has been with the organization for twenty-five years. That association oversees the programs of more than 430 high schools. Her vision, conviction, and leadership have been dedicated to helping schools in Minnesota reach their goals of providing equity for all students. McIntyre has been at the forefront of the issue from the beginning.

"Back in the early 1970s, it wasn't easy," McIntyre recalled. "At that stage we were battling a stereotype across the public spectrum that limited what women and girls could do in athletics. Young women today just can't believe the kinds of attitudes that females faced in those days. As leaders advocating change, we faced personal confrontation. I've seen many articles and received letters which had very unkind things to say because I was that woman out to ruin the boys' athletic programs, at least from their perspective.

"There was a strong belief that the boys' program had worked hard to get where it was at. They said, 'We've built the buildings, earned the support of booster clubs, what makes you think you should share in that?' And I can understand. If I had worked as hard as they did and somebody walked in and said I want half of it, I'd probably be a little defensive, too. But it was time to share. So when we got into the discussions of deciding how to share the gymnasiums and the seasons, it took some time and required some tough decision-makers."

Fortunately, the schools and their board of directors took action to ensure that the foundations were built on solid values, and that has made all the difference in Minnesota. The "Gender Equity in Athletics Manual" is an example of the results that have highlighted Minnesota as a leader in gender equity.

"In 1992 we realized that as schools were being examined by either the State Department of Education or the Office for Civil Rights, some schools were no longer familiar with what the laws and rules required. So we took the initiative to develop the manual for schools to use as they reviewed the status of their program. That has proven to be very helpful to our schools, because it is, as far as we know, one of the only resources which includes all of the information for which they are responsible. The manual clearly defines the process for conducting a review of their program, and it is up to them to lay out the plans for how they are going to come into compliance or stay in compliance.

"This manual represents our best understanding of what is expected of the schools," McIntyre confided. "And it has all the necessary information in one document. We have taken it down to a basic tenet: When one piece of the pie is left in the pan and two kids both want a piece, give one the knife to cut it in half and the other one gets first choice. That's equity in a pie-shell."

Other positive steps have been taken in the past few years to strengthen the cause for high school girls in interscholastic athletics. In late fall of 1993, continuing through 1994, Ocean Spray and the National High School Athletics Coaches Association sponsored the WAVE Program, or Women Athletes' Voice of Encouragement. The program was designed to encourage high school girls to participate in sports. Olympic gold medalist Summer Sanders was the spokeswoman the first year, and she toured the United

States speaking to high schools about the need to educate young women, as well as their parents and coaches, on the importance of participating in athletics. Sponsors also backed their cause with financial support to schools needing assistance in expanding or creating programs for girls.

The importance of this program was tremendous. WAVE was the first ever national, school-based program to support young women's high school athletics. Sanders's speaking tour provided the educational and motivational component while the sponsors, to borrow a cliché, put their money where their mouths were.

At the time, Sanders was the ideal candidate to lead off as WAVE spokeswoman. In the 1992 Summer Olympics held in Barcelona, Spain, she captured two gold medals, a silver, and a bronze with lifetime best performances in the 200-meter butterfly, 200- and 400-meter individual medleys, and the 4x100-meter medley relay.

"I'm trying to explain why girls should get involved in athletics, and it is not for the glory, first place, the gold medal or the world record," she explained. "That is not the real issue. It's being part of a team, experiencing failure, experiencing success, learning how to deal with that. It gives you confidence, and interacting with your peers out of the classroom in a different setting. The things they learn when they are working together with their team and creating goals are things they will use later on in life. Girls need to realize that they don't have to be afraid of failure. They have to realize they can take risks."

Sanders began swimming competitively at age four, competing against and defeating seven-year-olds. At fifteen, Sanders won a spot at the 1987 Olympic trials, but she missed qualifying for the 1988 games by 0.27 seconds. At Stanford University, she compiled six individual National Collegiate Athletic Association (NCAA) titles and four relay championships before trading her two remaining years of eligibility for endorsement contracts. She received back-to-back NCAA Swimmer of the Year honors, leading the Cardinal to the NCAA national championship as a sophomore.

Sanders was the beneficiary of something many high school girls do not receive. As a young girl growing up in Sacramento, California, Sanders had opportunity and encouragement. "I think our community really was unique," Sanders said. "It was very sports-conscious. We don't have any professional teams, except the Kings [of the National Basketball Association]. There were so many soccer programs for girls and boys and Little League. There was just an amazing number of opportunities for parents to get their kids involved in sports.

"When I started swimming and traveling a lot, I missed some school," Sanders went on. "My teachers in high school were very supportive, and the principal and vice principal were understanding."

Sanders's personal experience prompted her to jump at the chance to represent WAVE. She willingly signs autographs, but she felt that WAVE was a significantly better way to interact with young girls and share her views and recollections about athletics. Sanders also benefited from circumstances many high school girls are lacking.

"I think back to my years and career in swimming, I feel like I was real fortunate," Sanders said. "I've had a lot of motivation through my whole life. I had a lot of support from my family and my friends, my high school and my community in general. I know that there are a lot of young women out there who just don't have the motivation that I had, and so it's exciting for me to have the chance to give a little back by doing something more than just signing autographs . . . maybe motivate a few girls to experience all the great things that sports have to offer."

Studies show a variety of factors to explain the athletics participation drop-off in high school girls, and Sanders, through personal experience, can relate to some of those elements. That was another part of the educational wisdom she was able to impart during her speaking engagements.

"When I tell them all the hours I swam in high school, a lot of the girls wonder if I had a social life," Sanders said. "That is what a lot of them are worried about. Can I handle competing in athletics, go to school, and not miss out on all the parties, dances, and stuff. The whole point is they do not have to dedicate that much time to athletics [as I did to swimming]. If they decide that athletics is something they want to do, athletics is fun for them, I express to them it is possible to fit it all into one day. It is possible. I experienced that same thing, but I got it all in. I scheduled it all so I could do everything I wanted to do."

While Sanders was engaged in her speaking tour, Ocean Spray Cranberries distributed to the state executive secretaries of the National High School Athletic Coaches Association a WAVE package. In the package were ten applications for grants, awards, and scholarships. The state executive secretaries were asked to forward the materials to coaches or athletic directors in their state who should apply. The state executive secretaries were also encouraged to include announcements of the program in state newsletters or other publications.

Included in the packets were a cover letter to coaches describing WAVE, outlining the teaching elements provided to help coaches motivate young women to participate in sports and the scholarships and grants to support financially young women and high school sports programs. Coaches were offered two programs from which to select: the Ocean Spray/NHSACA WAVE Excellency Program or the Ocean Spray/NHSACA WAVE Grants Program.

The Excellency Program rewards high schools and coaches that are making outstanding efforts to increase young women's participation in sports. On the application, coaches were asked to describe what they and their schools were doing to increase women's participation in sports. Also, they were asked to describe what innovative programs were planned for the future that will continue to increase participation. In addition, coaches and schools were asked to demonstrate that participation in women's sports had increased over the previous two years. Finally, coaches were requested to nominate an outstanding student-athlete who deserved a scholarship.

The awards were generous. One national high school winner received a $10,000 Excellency Award, and one national student-athlete winner received a $10,000 scholarship over four years. Seven regional high school winners received $2,500 Excellency Awards, and seven regional student-athletes each received one-year $500 scholarships. Forty-three high school state winners received $750 Excellency Awards.

The WAVE Grants Program made awards to high schools and coaches who were in need of funding for women's sports. Schools and coaches were asked to describe specific needs of their women's sports programs which had not been implemented because of lack of funding. Also, coaches and schools were asked to describe how a WAVE grant would be utilized to encourage more young women to participate in sports. Again, coaches and schools were asked to nominate an outstanding student-athlete for a scholarship.

The grants mirrored the amounts awarded in the Excellence Program. The student-athlete scholarships were similar, as well, except the national winner, who received a $6,500 scholarship over four years.

The criteria for the student-athlete scholarships were difficult to meet: the student-athletes had to act as positive role models in nurturing younger players on the team; show a high degree of sportsmanship, enthusiasm, and dedication; be a team player; manage time well, such as successfully juggling schoolwork, extracurricular activities, jobs, and sports; plan an education beyond high school; have at least a 3.0 grade point average (on a 4.0 scale); and provide a quotation. The four-year scholarships for the national winners were awarded yearly over a four-year period for further education beyond high school, while the one-year scholarships applied to the first year for further education beyond the secondary level.

Ocean Spray's financial commitment to this program for one year totaled nearly $200,000, and if the endorsement fees for Sanders were added, the total financial commitment would be much greater. But funding was just one component of WAVE. The program also provided high school coaches with educational materials for working with young women. The education kit included a motivation video, coaches' activity guide, student magazine, and a parents' brochure.

Skip Colcord, manager of marketing communications for the Lakeville-Middleboro, Massachusetts, company, said that the WAVE program was a natural because it was consistent with Ocean Spray's image. "We've had a relationship with the Women's Sports Foundation for seven or eight years, and women are our primary consumer, so WAVE was a natural," Colcord explained. "No one else is promoting young women's involvement in high school athletics right now. This program is a good means for teaching teamwork, self-esteem . . . things women can carry with them for life. The feedback we have received so far has been all positive."

Dorothy McIntyre echoes the value of such supportive programs as WAVE. "I support programs which emphasize getting girls off the sidelines and into the action," McIntyre praised. "Using role models to be out front talking about benefits of participation for girls and women in sports sends a strong message to parents and students about the need to provide opportunities to participate.

"Girls and women need to feel welcome," McIntyre emphasized. "A prime example would be where one of our parks and recreation departments in Minneapolis could not understand why the middle school girls had dramatically dropped off in participation, but the boys were there in constant numbers. The parks and recreation people started going out to every school and speaking with the girls themselves. And they told the girls, we *want you* to come to the program. There is something here that *we would like you to be involved* in and you are going to have fun. The direct approach caused the program to blossom. What they found was, if they put up a sign-up sheet and said there will be something going on in the playground at one o'clock on Saturday, the boys will come. But girls want to know they are welcome.

"Women in all stages of society . . . fight for the right to be where they should be, but they also appreciate knowing that they are welcome. The worst thing is to get there and feel nobody wants you. Do we need more programs which support girls in sports and make them feel welcome . . . absolutely!"

Because of her success and experience as a world-class athlete, Sanders feels a certain responsibility to deliver the WAVE message. She also believes it is the responsibility of other champion women athletes to provide advocacy—not necessarily through WAVE but through other avenues as well. She also feels the young women she has been speaking with have an obligation as well.

"I've been expressing to a lot of the athletes in the assemblies that it is a responsibility for them as well," Sanders said. "They have to tell their peers, their friends, their classmates about it and get their friends involved in athletics . . . get the population in general more excited about women's athletics."

If only it were that easy.

4

Turf Wars

Each campus has to sit down and decide what are the purposes of intercollegiate athletics. If the purposes are to bring in money and to provide the largest PR arm for the university, then we have got to be up front and say, this is why we are doing it. If it is not the reason, then we have got to put it in an educational framework that makes sense. At least tell me what is the real purpose of intercollegiate athletics.

—Dr. Christine Grant,
Director of Women's Athletics, University of Iowa

Marilyn McNeil is the type of athletic director who haunts coaches of college football and men's basketball. McNeil was hired in April 1994 to oversee the athletic program at Monmouth College in West Long Branch, New Jersey. When she had been at the institution for less than a year, McNeil slashed the men's basketball budget by 30 percent, and she subtracted more than $150,000 from the men's football program, which operates under nonscholarship status.[1] McNeil did this in the name of gender equity. "I wanted to achieve fairness throughout the program," McNeil explained. "It was appalling to me to see the entire women's program with less of a budget than the men's basketball team alone, and even some of the other men's teams."

An analysis showed McNeil to be correct in her evaluation of the athletic budget; however, her solutions and methods have been scrutinized by the media, as well as by others in athletics. McNeil had genuine interests at heart but, perhaps, went about reaching her objectives in a less than logical manner.

Donna Lopiano, executive director of the Women's Sports Foundation, has an informal checklist for institutions to add women's teams as well as redistribute resources. Lopiano's first suggestion is to search for new money through fund-raising. Second, Lopiano recommends cutting items that don't affect the sports themselves, such as holding off on renovations or delaying plans for new construction. Third, Lopiano advises cutting middle management and similar items before the final step of cutting excesses in terms of a sport's standard of living or cutting teams.

Monmouth moved up to Division I basketball in 1983 by petitioning the NCAA for reclassification, and then applying Division I rules to its athletic program. This entailed increasing the minimum number of sports offered from eight to fourteen, increasing the amount of scholarship money offered to student-athletes, and adhering to stricter scheduling requirements as well as higher eligibility and academic standards.

Current coach Wayne Szoke took the reins nine years ago. During Szoke's tenure, the Hawks enjoyed six winning seasons in the last eight years, and went to the Northeast Conference (NEC) tournament championship game three times in the previous five seasons going into the 1995–1996 campaign. The winner of the NEC tournament earns an automatic bid to the NCAA tournament.

In the program's early years, the schedule was dotted with the likes of Georgetown, Georgia Tech, Villanova, and a host of other top teams, scheduled with the dual purpose of pocketing a nice check for serving as a guinea pig for the home team, and with the hopes that one of these opponents would stumble and fall, giving the fledgling program an instant boost of credibility. As the program progressed, the schedule became more manageable, the quality of the players began to improve, and Monmouth became a force in the NEC. Additionally, of the seven Division I basketball-playing schools in the Garden State, Monmouth had been a better draw than all, except Seton Hall, averaging more than 1,800 fans per home contest. That fan base has generated more than $20,000 in ticket sales each of the past few seasons.[2]

Football was added in 1993, and although it is not in the same league as state neighbors Rutgers or Princeton, the program generated $67,000 in revenue the first year and averaged between 4,000 and 5,000 fans per home game. The campus bookstore felt the spillover from the football team when it earned more than $30,000 during the fall alone from the sale of sweat-shirts, baseball caps, and T-shirts.[3]

Did McNeil do anything wrong by slashing the men's basketball budget? Perhaps she moved too far, too fast. Supporters say no, but some experts would not agree.

There are nine men's sports and eight women's sports at Monmouth. In 1994–1995, budgets were increased for men's baseball, track, golf, and tennis and for all eight women's sports. Forty-eight percent of the students are women, but only 38 percent of the student-athletes are women. Men's and women's basketball provide the school's only full scholarships: thirteen each. Overall, Monmouth offers 39 scholarships for women and 36.75 for men, or 51 percent of the scholarships go to women student-athletes.

Not only was the men's basketball budget slashed, but, more specifically, the recruiting segment of the budget was reduced from a meager $18,000 to a sparse $11,875, which is the same allotment for the women's basketball team.[4] McNeil claims, with her redistribution, that the women's budget was number one in the NEC, while the men's was third. Unnamed sources within the league say that Monmouth's men's budget was no better than seventh, including basketball.

The college also added women's lacrosse in the spring of 1995 and had plans to add another women's team in 1996. Monmouth also will have a brand new, reconstructed gymnasium floor and new bleachers.

Is it wise to jeopardize the only revenue-producing programs in the athletic department? College basketball recruiting experts, including Tom Konchalski, believe the cuts in the recruitment budget will do several things, none of them positive. Konchalski, editor and publisher of the recruiting newsletter HSBI Report, believes that Monmouth's recruiting reach, now extending from Boston to Baltimore, will be substantially diminished. Additionally, other recruiters have noted the absence of Monmouth's coaches from a number of summer camps that had been previously attended.[5] McNeil doesn't believe her budget cuts will have an adverse effect on the men's basketball or football program. But why take the chance?

"On the men's side, the per diems were as needed, but the judgment was by the coaches," McNeil countered. "They said, that's what we need, so that's what we are going to spend. There was no sense of how we traveled, how we came home, no principles involved. For example, if a coach was on a recruiting trip in Pittsburgh, Pennsylvania, instead of going on to Cleveland from there, he would come home first and then go to Cleveland.

"I looked at the number of coaches you could put on the road, the number of days you could be out on the road, the history of the athletes they brought in for visits. I scaled back the per diems, the campus visits and I calculated it as liberally as possible, and I still couldn't come up to $18,000. They did not need what they were spending. It was not responsible budgeting."

The crux of the situation is this. McNeil slashed the budget of an athletic program of which she was in charge for less than a year. She did not analyze or seek out new money through fund-raising. She admitted to not having a gender equity plan on paper at the time she made the budget cuts. Finally, a women's lacrosse team was added with a $20,000 budget, six partial scholarships, a full-time head coach, two paid assistants, and significant limitations.

There are only thirty-nine Division I women's lacrosse programs in the country, and lacrosse is not a popular sport offered in New Jersey high schools. Monmouth's travel expenses for both competition and recruiting will be higher than necessary and, reflecting on McNeil's assessment of the men's basketball budget, irresponsible. McNeil says the lacrosse decision was made prior to her being hired.

According to the National Federation of State High School Associations, women's lacrosse is not one of the top ten sports either offered by high schools in America or participated in by high school girls.[6] Monmouth does not have a women's volleyball team, and volleyball is the third most popular sport for high school girls, both in the number of high schools that offer it and in the number of participants. McNeil would personally like the next women's team to be crew, which makes sense since the college is located less than a football field from the ocean. Common sense might prevail, though, and the next women's team will probably be field hockey. The New Jersey shore area is a hotbed for high school field hockey, some of the best on the East Coast, and one of the unwritten requirements for adding new teams is to have a substantial recruiting base from which to draw.

At the birth of Monmouth's flight into Division I basketball, contributions from alumni and the community were commonplace and healthy. To think that McNeil did not explore this possibility is negligent. But McNeil, the former athletic director at California Polytechnic Institute, is noticeably uncomfortable with thoughts of glad-handing potential donors.

"You have to do it [fund-raising] as an athletic director," McNeil acknowledged. "I'm not real comfortable, nor am I very knowledgeable [about it] either. I have been to good golf tournaments, seen some great sponsorships, and I've done some good golf outings. I always see fund-raising as an opportunity to do something special, not to do something that's necessary. It's not for putting food on the table, it's for the ten-layer cake for dessert.

"What's the next piece?" McNeil asked rhetorically. "We are going to hire a marketing and development person for the first time. I want that person to be creative. I will be there for support, just like when I attend football games. I will be there to shake a hand if necessary, but if I am not needed, I can think of other things I can be doing."

Considering the lengths McNeil went to in order to redistribute the athletic budget and add one new team, the question arises about the funding source for the next women's team to be added. "I would hope the institution would give new money," McNeil said. "Every time we have a budget meeting, I bring up the fact that we will be adding a new women's team, and that has been acknowledged. Whether or not we get some [money], I don't know. No one knows, come budget time, what the crunch will be. I have a wonderful opportunity to sit with senior administrative staff and I get to keep athletics in the forefront in the budget process. I feel confident we won't get hurt in our other programs."

As for jeopardizing the quality of Monmouth's marquee program, McNeil doesn't believe there is any legitimacy to that claim. "I would be very concerned if it [the budget cuts] changed the quality of the team. I would not be terribly concerned about revenue generation, because basketball is not a revenue producer. There's no way I want to go backwards competitively. I want to leap forward, in fact, including men's basketball. I want to be at the top, and I think it can be done. We didn't have a great recruiting year in men's basketball, but as far as I know it wasn't because of a lack of money."

According to recruiting experts, Monmouth signed two players during the recruiting period, neither of which, allegedly, had any other scholarship offers from Division I institutions.

FOOTBALL FOLLIES

But such is the battle for fairness in intercollegiate athletics. Gender equity is seen as a threat to the standards many men's coaches have grown accustomed to over the years. College football's hierarchy has attacked gender equity with the tenacity of a blitzing linebacker facing fourth down at the one yard line.

College football throws a gargantuan monkey wrench into the entire gender equity process. By its nature, football has a participation rate that exceeds 100 participants at many institutions. Its costs are also enormous. To outfit a football player can cost more than $1,000, plus insurance, per diems for traveling, salaries for ten or more coaches, field maintenance, and so on. There is not one sport women play that can match football in participation numbers or expenditures. And that is the rub.

In order to achieve gender equity, many advocates recommend dipping into the football program to cut or cap participation or to cut scholarships further, thereby taking those funds and pouring them into increased opportunities for female student-athletes. Football coaches and other gridiron supporters point to football's revenue generation, its lucrative television contracts, and other intangibles in an attempt to stem the tide of "radical women" who want to damage the game. Football supporters contend that, because of football's revenue generation and because of the large number of participants, football should be given special consideration in the Title IX debate.

"The myth has been perpetuated as an excuse for not funding women's sports," said Donna Lopiano, executive director of the Women's Sports Foundation. "And the whole point is this. No one wants football not to be revenue producing—although it doesn't make enough to pay for itself in most places. The whole point is if sport is important enough to be in higher education and to receive the benefits of nonprofit status for the football boosters, then it is as important for girls to play as it is for boys. We shouldn't be choosing between our sons and daughters.

"And when you take it from that perspective, the issue is not cutting men's sports to provide for women," Lopiano continued. "The issue is maintaining current men's participation levels and bringing women up to their levels. And the only way we are going to do that is redistribute resources."

Campaigning and posturing of this sort are usually reserved for presidential elections, and then not usually executed as well. Both sides in this ongoing dispute have legitimate concerns and legitimate points of contention. One of the problems is that neither side wants to listen rationally to the other, and so this point-counterpoint continues.

The College Football Association (CFA) feels so strongly about its position that it threatened to pull out of the NCAA in June 1993 and form its own organization. Gender equity and, more specifically, the proportionality segment of the three-prong Office of Civil Rights test for Title IX compliance are the antagonists for the CFA. The CFA leaders contended that the NCAA could not afford to lose them as members and therefore would buckle under the threatened departure. The fact is Title IX is a federal law, not an NCAA mandate. Even if the CFA withdrew from the NCAA, it would not be exempt from Title IX. The CFA comprises the top sixty-seven Division I-A football programs in the country.

The CFA contends that college football is responsible for two-thirds of the income that finances athletics, yet direct expenditures for football (salaries, scholarships, equipment, recruiting, and travel) account for just 27 percent of the athletic expense budget.[7] Additionally, coaches complain that continued scholarship reductions for football will severely damage the product the coaches put on the field which attracts the lucrative television deals and revenue. The number of football scholarships that an institution can offer has been reduced over the last few years from 95 to 92 to 90 to 88 and now to 85. The scholarship cap for football in 1973 was 105.[8] Arguing against further scholarship cuts and participation caps, coaches reason that football is a developmental game where freshmen and sophomores are not physically or mentally prepared for competition, from five to ten players may be injured at any one time, and the National Football League now regularly drafts the top underclassmen, further depleting the ranks.

Jane Miller has been a member of the athletic department at the University of Virginia for thirteen years, and she is an associate athletic director, senior women's administrator, and former head coach of women's lacrosse. The Cavaliers' program is one of the more successful in the country, not only in victories and graduation rates, but in its treatment of the female student-athletes. Miller understands both sides of this sensitive debate.

"I think what's really important from a practical standpoint is you have to consider that your football and basketball programs are traditionally your revenue producers," Miller said. "You need to make sure that you protect those two entities and that you don't put them at a competitive disadvantage, which ultimately would impact all of the other programs. You have to be very careful in putting together your plan of action.

"I think this is an institutional issue, and there has to be a commitment from the top down," Miller went on. "It should be a carefully thought out process for your athletic department and the university. The intent is not to take away, it's to increase the opportunities for women and improve the quality of the athletic experience for all student-athletes. But the reality at some universities is that funds need to be reallocated and men's teams will be affected. So you have to go about the process in a very logical way for your university with a high emphasis on creating new resources so that, in the end, you are pleased with your program for both men and women."

Football partisans have two primary points of contention. The first is proportionality, the first part of the three-part test where football officials contend strict application of this test could lead to schools being found in violation even if a school offers the same amount of sports for both sexes and fewer women choose to participate.

The CFA is also banking on the Javits amendment, added to the Department of Education's rules on college athletics in 1974. In the amendment, Congress directed government regulators to consider that legitimate differences exist between men's and women's sports.[9] The American Football Coaches Association wants regulators to take the Javits amendment into account when dealing with football, which has an extraordinarily high participation rate and no comparable sport for women.

Title IX advocates have a different view on college football. According to the NCAA, of the 522 colleges and universities that offer football, only 58 (11 percent) generate enough revenue to cover costs.[10] According to the 1993 Revenues and Expenses of Intercollegiate Athletics report, 62 percent of Division I-A and I-AA football programs have, on the average, annual deficits of $1 million (for I-A) and $664,000 (for I-AA).[11] Additionally, women's proponents point to the NCAA statistics that show women student-athletes receive less than 24 percent of college athletic operating budgets, 18 percent of college recruiting budgets, and 28 percent of athletic scholarships.[12]

"There are approximately 25–30 percent of schools where the actual reality is football and then basketball do fund the rest of the men's and women's sports," said Christine Grant, director of women's athletics at the University of Iowa for twenty-three years. "That is true at Iowa; we are one of the very few schools that honestly can say that.

"But prior to 1970, the men's program had 100 percent of the financial resources of our university, and that was total discrimination," Dr. Grant continued. "They had both the moral and financial support of the university to promote and build a revenue-producing machine. Now because they had that advantage, past discrimination is now being used to justify current discrimination against women. That cannot be at an educational institution that has been mandated by the federal government to provide equal opportunity."

Consequently, to face the realities of this situation, college presidents and athletic directors have developed methods to deal with these circumstances. Rather than slash football and men's basketball operations, the solutions usually have been to reduce or eliminate men's nonrevenue teams, such as gymnastics, swimming, wrestling, and tennis. According to the NCAA, in the 1974–1975 academic year, the NCAA had 704 members: 401 offered wrestling; 133, men's gymnastics. In 1994–1995, with 909 member institutions, 261 sponsored wrestling and 32 offered men's gymnastics.[13]

Eliminating men's sports has become an easy way for some college presidents and athletic directors to acquiesce to Title IX. Unfortunately, eliminating men's teams contradicts the purpose of Title IX, and that is to improve and enhance opportunities for women through increased participation opportunities and additional scholarships. Eliminating men's teams often is an attempt to make the percentages even out in the proportionality test, but without the addition of opportunities for female student-athletes, this solution falls short of the objective. It also creates a barrier between the men's and women's programs—a separation usually flavored with animosity.

The hostility would not be there if each side would recognize the basic facts. According to an NCAA study on sex equity, men's teams receive 70 percent of athletic scholarship money, 77 percent of the operating budget, and 83 percent of the recruiting money at large Division I-A institutions. Although the total enrollment at all institutions is virtually equal, male student-athletes outnumber female student-athletes by more than two to one.[14]

In a 1993 study done by the National Association of College and University Business Officers (NACUBO), 70 percent of Division I athletics programs lost money in 1989. Less than 100 schools made money.[15] However, according to the NCAA, even though only about 30 percent of Division I athletics programs bring in more than they spend, football still contributes the most revenue, nearly 50 percent at Division I-A schools.[16]

Does football have value for an intercollegiate athletic program? Rhetorical question. Can football tighten the fiscal belt loops in order to eliminate some of the discriminatory advantages currently enjoyed? Absolutely.

Title IX advocates must realize that most, if not all, intercollegiate athletic programs were built almost a century ago with football as the foundation, and perhaps as the only team offered for a number of years. Football was the first sport that elevated the visibility and exposure and enhanced the prestige and image of institutions. Notre Dame is a good example. Football also attracted alumni contributions (unfortunately for some schools) and, at state schools, encouraged legislative support. An economics professor at Boston College claimed applications to the school increased 30 percent the year Doug Flutie led the Eagles to their Cinderella upset of Miami in 1985.[17]

"I think that is a normal human response," said Dr. Grant regarding football's resistance. "I think if you have been used to certain standards of living and you have enjoyed that particular standard of living, you are going to fight tooth and nail to make sure it doesn't change. And I don't care if you are talking about men or women. That would be the natural response.''

Football has continued to enjoy a charmed lifestyle at many Division I institutions, as well as the more successful programs on the lower levels. Football coaches have grown accustomed to first-class treatment: first-class equipment, plush offices, cavernous training facilities, royal travel accommodations, and a variety of perks. Many coaches, also in men's basketball, have clauses in their contracts for post-season bonuses and additional rewards for national championships. Should coaches be compensated extra for guiding a team to superior status? Why not? Any good company salesman receives a bonus for extraordinary performance. However, the company is not, in good conscience, going to jeopardize the business or alienate other employees by rewarding that salesman with an exorbitant bounty.

Football coaches perceive their livelihood to be threatened with the aggressive approach of Title IX and gender equity proponents. Their concerns are legitimate and understandable. Their scholarship allotment has steadily dwindled over the past few years, but excesses still exist in many of the larger Division I-A programs, particularly the CFA membership. It is common practice at a number of institutions for the football team to be lodged in a hotel the night before a *home* game. Coaches fly recruits in for a campus visit, a recruit they might not be interested in, just so a rival institution doesn't have the opportunity of the visit. Some coaches fly, probably first class, to and from a campus visit with a recruit, basically wasting three round-trip tickets. What might the costs add up to for any of these unnecessary practices? Enough to fund another women's team? Perhaps a half dozen scholarships for the women's program? How much does it cost to house a football squad of approximately 100 players and ten coaches for one night?

"One of the advantages I had was being in the position I was and being able to see things differently than I had in the past," said Merrily Dean Baker, former athletic director at Michigan State. "For years I targeted that single issue of having the football team stay off campus the night before a game as one of the major sins of college sports. I now view that particular issue very differently. I now understand why the coach has it or wants to have it. I didn't know that until I lived on the campus this size in a town this size and saw what happens in this town on Friday night. I lived through a year of a number of athletes getting arrested for missteps, being goaded into things, and being harassed.

"However, like everything else, it's all or nothing," Baker continued. "I think there are ways to reduce the cost of that housing. It doesn't have to be all 140 people on the squad that stay there. It might be your top 30 players. Michigan State does not house the players off campus. It has a facility on campus from the hotel school and that is where the team stays. There are a lot of ways to cut back. We have a lifestyle in athletics we can no longer sustain. It's a hard sell, though, when you have a myopic view of men's athletics and the value of them."

Football can make some financial sacrifices that will not damage the quality of the teams, threaten alumni donations, or jeopardize television exposure or revenue generation. Additionally, it is extremely difficult to believe that fair-minded men like Penn State's Joe Paterno or Nebraska's Tom Osborne would deny female student-athletes an opportunity to participate in athletics. They wouldn't. They simply don't want gender equity to jeopardize the programs they have built over the past twenty years.

"We had a 20th anniversary for our program," Dr. Grant said. "We invited back as many student-athletes as we could contact. What struck me the entire weekend was what successful and wonderful young women we have helped produce. The reason some people have strongly opposed opportunity for women in sports is they perceive women as being weak and helpless and passive. What does sports do? It does exactly the opposite. It produces women who are very strong, competent, assertive, confident with high self-esteem. So we actually shatter the myth that some people in society want to continue. That is one of the huge lessons sports can give to young women who are trying to find their role in society on an equal basis with their brothers."

Title IX advocates have rightful concerns as well. This federal law is nearly twenty-five years old, and still approximately 90 percent of all colleges and universities are not in compliance. The battle cry is "Why should we wait any longer, we've already waited twenty years?" Twenty years too long.

COURTS OF FLAWS

Unfortunately, a number of obstacles have been virtual roadblocks to the success of this legislation. Many wonder why it took so long for Title IX to be enforced as rigorously as it has been during the past five years.

Congress passed Title IX to the Education Amendments on June 23, 1972. The compliance date for elementary schools was set for July 1976; high schools and colleges had until 1978. It wasn't, however, until 1979 that the Department of Health, Education and Welfare (HEW) issued its policy interpretation, one year after the compliance date for colleges and high schools and three years after the deadline for grammar schools.

While many athletic programs, at all levels, experienced phenomenal growth during the mid to late 1970s, the law hit its second barrier in 1984. Grove City College of Pennsylvania, in *Grove City v. Bell*, argued that Title IX applied only to those departments within an institution of higher education that actually received federal funds. The Supreme Court ruled that the punishment for Title IX infractions, loss of those federal funds, applied only to those specific departments receiving federal funds, not the college in general. Thus, since athletic departments did not directly receive federal funds, they were exempt from the Title IX mandate. Fortunately, in 1988, Congress addressed this situation in the Civil Rights Restoration Act and ruled that, if one part of an educational institution received federal funds, the entire institution, all departments, were responsible for Title IX compliance.

"The Civil Rights Restoration Act brought Title IX off the back burner, and lawsuits began to be listened to," said Baker. "In the intervening years, HEW or OCR [Office of Civil Rights] really hadn't done much. They sat on their haunches and, if someone complained, they would go out and follow up on the complaint. The bottom line was inconsistent answers were given in every region of the country. The bottom line was unless someone filed a complaint, they [the agency] didn't conduct any monitoring. What we had was a series of colleges and universities, for the first fifteen to seventeen years, that said we will just wait and see if we get hit . . . if we don't, we won't do anything. And that is a rather strong statement."

Although Title IX was passed in 1972, because of the delay by HEW in issuing its policy interpretation and then the Grove City decision in 1984, Title IX realistically didn't get untracked until 1988. Again, though, as recently as July 1995, the federal government was once again shooting itself in the foot, this time at the bequest of college football coaches and coaches of nonrevenue men's sports. Because of the vehement protests lodged by the CFA and other organizations, Congressional hearings were held to determine the fairness and appropriateness of Title IX and, more specifically, the three-prong test authored by the Office of Civil Rights.

A U.S. House of Representatives subcommittee passed an amendment that would eliminate funds to the Department of Education's Office of Civil Rights to enforce Title IX legislation in intercollegiate athletics until that agency had released "objective criteria" explicitly detailing how institutions can comply with the second and third portions of the OCR compliance test. During the oversight hearing, members of the House stated that there exists "a lack of clarity as to how to show compliance." The proposed amendment, part of an education funding bill for fiscal 1996, must pass the House, Senate, and the president.[18] Here is another barricade, another delay.

But the OCR and, more specifically, the three-prong compliance test are really at the heart of this standoff. The Office of Civil Rights of the U.S. Department of Education is the principal government agency in charge of enforcing Title IX. Title IX covers three primary areas of interscholastic and intercollegiate athletics: financial assistance, accommodation of interest and abilities, and other athletic program elements.

The basis of the law says that the benefits, opportunities, and treatment of each sex must be essentially equal. That does not mean, however, that it must be identical. For example, football equipment and field hockey equipment have different costs, but the quality must be the same. Budgets do not have to be equivalent. The level of services provided to each program must be the same. However, if one gender has benefits greater than the other, an institution has three choices: it can increase benefits for the underrepresented gender, decrease the benefits of the overrepresented gender, or a little of both.

The first portion of the OCR test is for proportionality. To determine compliance with this first prong, the OCR compares the number of male and female student-athletes with the number of full-time male and female students in the overall student body. If the ratios are close, the school is probably in compliance with part one of the test. Institutions must be careful not to count the number of teams for each gender. Since teams have varying numbers of participants, the actual number of participants must be gauged, not the number of teams. Since the average NCAA institution has a ratio of approximately 66 percent male student-athletes and 33 percent female student-athletes, compared to the average student body ratio of 50–50, most NCAA institutions fail this segment of the OCR review.

The second prong of the OCR review states that institutions must demonstrate a history and continuing practice of program expansion for the underrepresented gender. Another way to comply would be for an institution to show it has increased opportunities as well as resources over the past five to ten years, is in the midst of implementing a plan to add new women's teams, or has a plan of action in place displaying its intentions to increase opportunities in the immediate future.

Finally, an institution can comply by fully and effectively accommodating the interests and abilities of the underrepresented gender. An institution must determine, through a self-analysis, if there are teams it doesn't offer that it should. It isn't enough for a young woman and three of her friends to say they want to compete in gymnastics or field hockey. There must be a satisfactory number of interested participants to sustain a competitive team, and there must be a sensible expectation that the new team can find competition within logical geographical parameters. In other words, it might not be wise to initiate a new women's team if no other school in the conference, or within a two-hour bus trip, has a varsity team in the same sport.

When the three-part OCR compliance test is scrutinized, the arguments from football coaches and others seem unfounded. The hang-up with the CFA and its constituents is the proportionality test. Institutions need satisfy only *one* of the three parts of the OCR test to be found in compliance.

Instead of being hamstrung on proportionality, football coaches and their fraternity brothers should be participating in the development of new women's teams. What would it take to start a women's soccer team? Twenty less players on the football traveling team? Seventy-five less players staying in the off-campus hotel the night before a home football game? Or a football staff donating its Sugar Bowl bonus to fund scholarships for female student-athletes?

And coaches of men's teams cannot accurately say that Title IX has meant subtraction for participation opportunities for male student-athletes. While some institutions do elect to eliminate some men's teams in order to comply with the law, NCAA statistics show that the number of male intercollegiate athletes increased by 16,000 between 1982 and 1992.[19]

Donna Lopiano explained:

> It's [proportionality] very clear and it's the only possible way to interpret the law. People don't realize there is a fine line of opportunities available in college sports. There are approximately 186,000 males and a little more than 100,000 women participating. There are millions of kids playing in high school. There are ten times as many kids who would play were you to offer the team at the college level. There is not a lack of interest in playing college sports, there is a lack of resources. Institutions have one choice. Do you make the same resources available to females as you do for males? The only way to prove that nobody is interested is to offer a team and have nobody come.

Baker concurs with Lopiano's assessment, but she identifies a critical point. "Proportionality is the first step, but that is a separate issue from the finances. To simply say the finances ought to be in the same proportion is being a little naive. We have not yet dealt with the reality of football, and we have to figure a way to include that in the formula. The reality is when you have a hundred young men in a sport that requires expensive equipment and expensive facilities, you can't compare it to the women's swimming team.

"What we have missed all these years is a way to determine a needs-based approach," Baker continued. "You need to identify what is needed to operate each of those sports. Where the commitment comes in is that you provide equally for those needs. The needs of the football team are going to be different from those of the women's swimming team, but they each ought to have their needs fully met in order to have a chance to be successful."

Institutions that field a football team are at a disadvantage with the first part of the OCR test, and coaches and administrators have voiced their concerns over this aspect. Additionally, coaches from grammar school through college argue with the second and third parts of the OCR test, questioning whether girls are as interested in sports as boys are. One Division I-A women's administrator even said it is hard for her to imagine that 50 percent of the population, that females, are as interested in sports as males. She went on to say that people have to realize that little girls like to play with Barbie dolls and do other things. Additionally, according to statistics, 64 percent of high school senior varsity athletes are male. In 1993–1994, according to the National Federation of State High School Associations, boy participants in varsity sports outnumbered girl participants by 3,478,530 to 2,124,755.[20]

Is counting heads an effective measuring stick for this federal mandate? Opponents insist that implementing new women's teams and proportionality must be linked to interest, and interest should be measured before taking any steps. Advocates argue interest studies are inaccurate. Interest cannot be measured in something that hasn't previously been offered.

"If the opportunities are there you are going to find women who will take them," said Virginia's Miller. "They will seize them. Not only for the experience of participating in a sport in which they enjoy, but also for the potential impact on their careers. Recruiters from major corporations in the country come to our campus and they want to interview women student-athletes because of all the extra benefits they derive from their athletic experiences. Time after time former student-athletes come back and express the positive impact their athletic experiences have had on their careers and lives. Both men and women receive those same benefits from a quality athletic experience."

In an attempt to develop a gauge by which institutions can measure interest, the NCAA Research Committee developed a survey vehicle that is being tested at institutions representing all NCAA classifications: Long Beach University, North Dakota State, Washburn University of Topeka, and the University of Wisconsin-LaCrosse. The expectations are for this test to distinguish interest levels between intramurals, club, and varsity.

Creating additional confusion with Title IX and gender equity are the other program areas the law touches. In addition to participation opportunities, Title IX addresses such elements as financial assistance, equipment and supplies, scheduling of games and practice times, travel per diems, access to tutoring, the quality of coaching, locker rooms, practice and competitive facilities, publicity, recruiting . . . the list goes on.

In an attempt to solve the turmoil, the NCAA, in 1992, appointed the Gender Equity Task Force. This group comprised twenty-four people from various NCAA disciplines as well as a number of outside consultants. The committee issued its final report in May 1993, but many gender equity advocates were disappointed with the results.

The task force was to define gender equity, advise institutions on how to comply, and suggest steps the NCAA could take to assist institutions in achieving compliance. It primarily stood behind the existing Title IX legislation, touting proportionality as the ultimate goal. It also suggested that institutions who have conducted a self-study to also develop an action plan to address the findings. Additionally, the task force determined that maintaining the revenue capability of football and men's basketball, as well as enhancing the revenue-generation capabilities of women's teams, was paramount to increasing opportunities for women.

Specifically, the task force defined gender equity in the following statement: "An athletics program is gender equitable when either the men's or women's sports program would be pleased to accept as its own the overall program of the other gender."

Title IX supporters were disgruntled because they felt the task force didn't go far enough. It was felt that there wasn't enough impetus to force institutions to comply, nor were any penalties set forth for noncompliance. It's a difficult dilemma. Since Title IX is a federal law, does the task force, and ultimately the NCAA, have the right or obligation to penalize institutions for noncompliance?

"It failed miserably in terms of creating an incentive system, either a penalty system or some way that they could really correct the issue," said

Lopiano. "It would be easy for the NCAA to say, you can't become a member unless you are doing this or you can't get into the championships unless you are doing this. But it is simply not willing to bust the establishment to do that."

The task force basically accomplished what it was charged with, and it did provide some significant suggestions. The task force recommended increasing the maximum financial aid limitations for some Division I-A and II women's sports, specifically increasing scholarships in women's soccer, field hockey, and lacrosse. It also suggested expanding women's NCAA championships to a level comparable with men. Another key advisement was for institutions, conferences, and the NCAA itself to include women, with greater frequency, in the decision-making process.

To accomplish these goals, the task force recommended each institution have a senior women's administrator (SWA), increase the appointments of female faculty athletics representatives, increase the number of females on athletics councils and boards, and increase the ratio of female representatives on NCAA committees.

The task force came to a number of intelligent conclusions. Self-analysis and plans of action are strongly recommended. To date, any institution that has gone to court to defend against a Title IX suit has lost. The judicial system has varied views of Title IX, as displayed by numerous court decisions over the past few years. An institution that believes it is in compliance could find out otherwise in a court of law. Additionally, litigating court cases is costly, in terms both of money and image. Just ask the administrators from Brown University or a number of others who have not fared successfully in defending Title IX suits.

In legal terms, *Franklin v. Gwinnett County Public Schools* could be the most important court decision regarding a Title IX case. In this 1992 case, the court awarded, for the first time, monetary damages to the plaintiffs because the discriminatory acts were found to be intentional.

However, the case between Brown University and a number of former female student-athletes is the most publicized and, for many, the most significant example. In May 1991, Brown administrators announced, because of budgetary constraints, it was eliminating funding for four varsity athletic teams: women's gymnastics and volleyball and men's golf and water polo. Brown also stated the teams could continue to compete as intercollegiate clubs. By permitting the four teams to continue competition as clubs, this status enabled those teams to compete against varsity clubs from other institutions, but without funding and support, such as salaried coaches, access to facilities, preferred practice time, medical trainers, office support, and so on. Members of both women's teams filed a class-action suit, and a federal trial court issued an injunction forcing Brown to reinstate both women's sports at the varsity level.[21]

The university appealed, and in April 1993, the U.S. Court of Appeals for the First Circuit upheld the lower court's ruling. Brown argued that the court relied exclusively on the first part of the three-part OCR test and ignored the other two parts. Brown also argued that it met two of the three parts of the OCR compliance standards, claimed its percentage of female student-athletes was 45 percent, and noted that the amount of teams it offered was significant.[22] Brown argued that it met Title IX compliance because of its history of expansion for the women's athletic program, but the court rejected that claim. While it recognized Brown's vigorous development in women's athletics in the 1970s, it also noted there had been a twelve-year lull in its efforts.[23]

On part three, Brown argued that, even though its participation numbers were not proportionate, it didn't fully meet the needs of its male athletes and therefore was not obligated to fully meet the needs of its female student-athletes either. The court stated that its treatment of its male student-athletes, did not constitute a legal reason for ignoring the needs of its female student-athletes.[24]

Before the proposed cuts, women's participation at Brown was 36.7 percent (36.6 with proposed cuts), and the men's percentage actually rose from 63.3 percent to 63.4 percent. At the time of the suit, Brown's student body was 52 percent male and 48 percent female.[25] Sensing the advantage, the lawyers for the female student-athletes not only wanted the two teams cut to be reinstated, but also wanted women's club teams in fencing, skiing, and water polo elevated to varsity status.

Ironically, Brown University is considered a leader in opportunities for women's athletics. The university offers seventeen varsity sports for women and sixteen varsity teams for men. According to some athletic directors, Brown offers more female athletic teams than almost any other institution of higher education, except Stanford. According to NCAA statistics, the average amount of women's teams offered by colleges and universities is approximately 8.3, and Brown's female participation level is approximately three times the national average.[26] However, only approximately 342 women participate, while approximately 555 men do.[27]

The case went to trial in the fall of 1994. The university settled part of the dispute by agreeing to provide comparable treatment and support to its male and female athletes for at least three years in areas such as coaching, recruiting, equipment, and facilities. Both sides agreed Brown had made significant improvements in its women's program in recent years, and that it was already providing essentially equitable treatment. This settlement, according to both sides, would anchor those commitments.[28]

The other part of the court case remains unsettled. In March 1995, U.S. District Court judge Raymond Pettine gave Brown 120 days to come up with a plan to comply with Title IX, stating, essentially, that many more men enjoy the benefits of varsity athletics competition than do women at the university. In his sixty-nine-page decision, he noted that, in the 1993–1994 academic year, 38 percent of the student-athletes at Brown were women while the undergraduate enrollment was 51 percent female.[29]

The judge left it up to the university to decide how it would comply. He said that the institution could eliminate its athletics program altogether, it could increase its number of female athletes, or it could cut opportunities for male athletes. Pettine discounted interest surveys the university provided regarding the third part of the OCR test, but cited enough interest that the university could sponsor women's teams in gymnastics, fencing, skiing, and water polo.

In August 1995, Brown sent a proposal to Judge Pettine for his review. The plan offered to cut men's sports and expand women's opportunities by creating more junior varsity teams. Pettine ruled that this plan was not acceptable and that the institution would still be in violation of Title IX. School officials insisted that they would continue their appeal efforts.[30]

What is really at the heart of the matter is a court of law deciding how a university will allocate its resources. The university, a proud Ivy League institution, has decided that that is unacceptable. Of course, Brown, in the eyes of the common man, has already shot itself in the foot. In arguing for the proposed cuts in its athletics program because of financial reasons, the institution has contradicted itself. Brown could easily have taken the money it has spent on the trial and have funded a number of women's teams, along with the requisite equipment and financial aid allotment.

The officials at Indiana University of Pennsylvania (IUP) can sympathize with Brown. The court in this case similarly ruled that the university could not determine its own course and decide which women's athletic teams to sponsor in order to comply. In the case of *Favia v. IUP*, again, the school announced it would cut women's gymnastics and field hockey and men's soccer and tennis because of budgetary reasons. Prior to the proposed cuts, 55 percent of the students were female, but only 37 percent of the student-athletes were female. After the proposed cuts, the women's participation rate would have dropped to 36 percent. Members of both women's teams filed a class-action suit.[31]

The court ruled that IUP didn't meet any of the three parts of the compliance test. University officials didn't appeal the court's decision to reinstate the programs, but they appealed to the court to allow the university to substitute women's soccer for gymnastics. When the court denied their request, university officials appealed to the U.S. Court of Appeals for the Third Circuit.[32]

If any institution had the preposterous notion of gaining a legal victory, the decision by this court should serve notice—even if the institution had a legitimate proposal. The Third Circuit acknowledged that substituting soccer for gymnastics made sense. It would help alleviate the Title IX violation because it would create more opportunities for women to participate, raising the percentage of female student-athletes from 37 to 43 percent. And since a gymnastics team would cost approximately $100,000 a year more than a women's soccer team, the court also stated this would make more funds available for other women's programs. After making these statements, however, the court refused to overturn the lower court's ruling. So much for institutional autonomy.[33]

In the *Cook v. Colgate University* case, the U.S. District Court for the Northern District of New York distinguished itself as being the only court to determine a case based on other components in the athletic program. Colgate administrators were petitioned by the women's ice hockey club team for varsity status four times: in 1979, 1983, 1986, and 1988. All four times the university denied the request. Former members of the team filed a suit, but not a class-action suit. Although Colgate sponsors the same number of sports for both genders, the men's athletic budget ($380,861) exceeded the women's program ($218,970). The court found Colgate in violation and ordered it to elevate the sport to varsity status.

Colgate officials argued that there was an inability to field a team—the absence of an NCAA championship, lack of competition, lack of student interest, and lack of talent—and added that the team would be a financial burden. It was found, however, that there were sufficient women ice hockey players to field a team, that there were sixteen other varsity women's ice hockey programs in the region, that having an NCAA championship is not a prerequisite to fielding a varsity team, and so on.[34]

Finally, in the *Roberts v. Colorado State Board of Agriculture*, an institution finally challenged the court's authority. Colorado State University (CSU) announced it was discontinuing women's softball (eighteen participants) and men's baseball (fifty-five participants). The U.S. Court of Appeals for the Tenth Circuit found CSU had violated Title IX because it failed to accommodate effectively the interests and abilities of its female students-athletes.

The court ordered the reinstatement of the program. Although CSU had added eleven women's sports in the 1970s, the court found the women's programs suffered more in budget cuts (34 percent) over the past twelve years than the men's program (20 percent). Additionally, the court found that, whereas CSU's student body was 48.2 percent female, only 37.7 percent of its student-athletes were.

CSU officials petitioned the Supreme Court to review the lower court's ruling and asked the Supreme Court to determine whether the lower court exceeded its authority by ordering CSU to immediately and permanently reinstate a specific athletic program rather than allow the university to determine its own course of action in order to comply with Title IX. The Supreme Court refused to review the case.[35]

"I think there are two things that are happening," said Iowa's Dr. Grant. "Administrators are getting a message loud and clear that they have got a choice. They can either voluntarily provide the opportunities or they are going to go to court, and that is going to be a more expensive route. That is why we are starting to see schools say we are strongly considering adding another sport. They are trying to keep a half step ahead of the law.

"These young student-athletes across the nation are talking to each other, it's like an informal network is starting to be built," Dr. Grant continued. "They are talking to each other, and I have been really surprised. These young women are saying enough is enough, either do it voluntarily or we'll see you in court."

Some institutions have decided that court isn't the best place to settle a Title IX dispute. And, in fact, they have decided to spend their resources in a more fruitful manner. In an unwritten message to their brethren, the University of Texas (Austin) and Auburn University both recently settled Title IX cases without going to court. One would be hard pressed to find people more passionate about football than the folks in Alabama and Texas; nonetheless, these two institutions took a proactive approach to their shortcomings.

In *Sanders v. University of Texas*, female students filed a class-action suit in July 1992 alleging the university did not accommodate the interests and abilities of its female students. The female students wanted the university to bring the number of athletics opportunities closer to the proportion of females in the student body. Women represented 47 percent of the student body, represented 23 percent of the student-athletes, and received 33 percent of the athletic scholarships. The students wanted four women's club teams—crew, softball, gymnastics, and soccer—elevated to varsity status.

A year later, without litigation, Texas agreed to raise women's participation from 23 percent to 44 percent, or within 3 percent of the 47 percent female undergraduate enrollment, within three years. The university also agreed to add women's varsity soccer in 1993–1994 and women's varsity softball in 1995–1996. Additionally, the university committed itself, after a five-year phase-in period, to increase women's athletic scholarships from 32 percent to 42 percent.

In addition to adding the two teams and committing to adding scholarships, the institution planned to increase the number of female walk-ons and decrease the number of male walk-ons. The changes will cost the university more than $1 million per year, and university officials said the costs will be met through fund-raising, cost cutting, and an increase in student fees.[36]

In *Kiechel v. Auburn University*, the university went beyond the demands stated in the suit. Female students filed a class-action suit to have the university upgrade women's club soccer to varsity status. The university agreed to do so and also committed $400,000 to women's varsity soccer for operating expenses in the 1993–1994 and 1994–1995 academic years, agreed to construct permanent practice and game fields for use by the start of the 1994 season, agreed to phase in scholarships at a predetermined rate, and paid damages plus attorney's fees and expenses.[37] Do it right, or don't do it at all.

"When you look at the Auburn case and the Texas case you are looking at major football powers who have just said, my lawyers have told me that this is a real waste of money . . . try to get out with your shirt and do something that has good public relations value," said Lopiano. "And they are making the move. I think that is a significant turnaround because what we don't need at this point is for these major football schools to pull a Custer's Last Stand and give everybody the stall incentive."

JOB OPENING: WOMEN NEED NOT APPLY

While female student-athletes are winning the day in court, and opportunities are increasing, other sectors of women's intercollegiate athletics are in peril.

During the week of February 10, 1995, Merrily Dean Baker resigned as athletic director at Michigan State University (MSU)—a sad and quick departure from the athletics business for a talented, intelligent, and qualified individual. In 1992 Baker became only the second woman to hold the athletic director position at a Division I institution competing in the top two revenue-producing sports: men's basketball and football. Barbara Hedges at the University of Washington is the other. Baker also became the first woman athletic director in the Big Ten Conference. Regardless of gender, Baker is highly qualified for the Michigan State post, or any other for that matter.

Prior to her brief stay in East Lansing, Baker had been an assistant executive director with the NCAA for four years, was director of women's athletics at the University of Minnesota for six years, and was the associate director for men's and women's athletics at Princeton University for twelve years. Baker actually initiated the women's sports program at Princeton.

Baker took over for former Spartans football coach George Perles, who had also served as interim athletic director for two years prior to Baker's hire. John DiBiaggio, the president of the university at the time, had been at odds with Perles over his dual role as athletic director and head football coach. DiBiaggio left MSU the day after Baker's arrival, and Baker's stay at MSU was never pleasant thereafter. Critics claimed Baker was too inexperienced to operate a Division I program and lacked the power base to make difficult decisions, especially without Dr. DiBiaggio on campus.

"There was tremendous controversy over George [Perles] being removed from the athletic director's position," explained Baker. "And I walk in, as a somewhat innocent lamb. I didn't come here naively, don't misunderstand me. I looked at the situation very, very carefully. But, at any rate, I walked in, before anyone even met me, knowing there was going to be a group here that was going to try to get me out of here. And there was a small group there that was trying to get me out before I even arrived."

An analysis of Baker's resumé prior to going to East Lansing shows the critics' objections were unfounded. Additionally, a review of the manner in which Perles used the threat of coaching opportunities in the National Football League as a bargaining chip to enhance his position with MSU, as well as the fact that Perles's teams did not achieve much more than mediocrity, shows the allegiance shown him by boosters and alums was idiotic. Perles was dismissed as head football coach following the 1994–1995 season.

In 1994 Baker was stripped of her control of football, men's basketball, and men's ice hockey, the three primary revenue-producing sports for Spartans athletics. School officials would not call it what it was—an abomination—but rather chose the politically correct route. School officials claimed the move was to free Baker up to work on fund-raising, marketing, promotion, and other challenges facing the MSU athletic department.

Clarence Underwood, associate athletic director for compliance and student affairs for five previous years, was promoted to senior associate athletic director to handle football, men's basketball, and ice hockey. Associate athletic director Kathy Lindahl remained responsible for Michigan State's other twenty-two sports.

Having been essentially deemed a lame duck the previous year, it was not a surprise Baker "resigned." Regarding her resignation, MSU president Peter McPherson said the decision had been a mutual one and that Baker would be paid for the remaining two years of her contract—a noble gesture, but actually nothing more than a poor attempt at public relations.

Baker's plight is an example of the female journey into athletic administration. At the time of Baker's resignation in February 1995, there were just four female athletic directors at NCAA Division I institutions, just two of whom, Barbara Hedges at the University of Washington and Debbie Yow at the University of Maryland, conducted high-profile programs.[38]

"It is flat out the effects of the old boys' club," Baker said. "It is an area of change that has been very slow to come, and it is almost the last male bastion, if you will. By that I mean the old-fashioned male bastions. It is a different kind of club and they haven't wanted to admit women. It has been difficult, but the world is changing. It's awful that there are so few women in high administrative positions."

In August 1994, Debbie Yow became the first female athletic director in the Atlantic Coast Conference, and just the fourth of 106 Division I programs that play football. With Suzanne Tyler as the senior associate athletic director, Maryland is the only Division I institution with women in the top two athletics administrative positions.[39] According to a report by Brooklyn University professors Vivian Acosta and Linda Carpenter, 21 percent of women's collegiate programs are run by women, up from 16.8 percent in 1992. It is significantly lower, however, than in 1972, when 90 percent of women's programs were run by women administrators. In 1986 the association hit the all-time low of 15.2 percent.[40]

"We do not have a commitment from the people who are supposed to be leaders of our institutions of higher learning," said Iowa's Dr. Grant. "There is no commitment to search out and appoint qualified women.

"In the early seventies, when men's and women's programs were separate, more than 90 percent of female athletic programs were administered by a woman," Grant continued. "When the merger between men's and women's athletics took place, and it was a forced merger in many instances, institutions selected men to be the athletic directors and women were frozen out."

Still, modest advances continue. In December 1992, when Constance H. Hurlbut was selected to become the executive director of the Patriot

League, she became the first woman to oversee an all-sport Division I conference for men and women. In 1994 Linda M. Bruno was appointed commissioner of the Atlantic 10 Conference. Bruno was the former associate commissioner of the Big East Conference and chairwoman of the NCAA Division I Women's Basketball Committee. When Yow was appointed at Maryland, she became the first woman to be named athletic director at two different Division I institutions; she had already served for four years in that capacity at Saint Louis University. There are thirteen women athletic directors out of 302 institutions that compete at the Division I level.[41]

For Hurlbut, the transition has been rather smooth. Hurlbut spent seven years prior to the Patriot League position in the Ivy League office as an assistant commissioner and associate director, and prior to the Ivy League, she was an assistant commissioner with the Eastern College Athletic Conference. The Patriot League has been a football conference since 1986, but had been an all-sports league for only four years before Hurlbut's appointment.

"My reception has been very positive," the University of Pennsylvania grad said. "I've found that attitudes about women in athletics and women in real leadership positions on campuses are changing. It is not unusual that a male coach reports to a female administrator. Consequently, the idea of having a female commissioner is not that unusual."

As many of her predecessors have done, Hurlbut stares at the reality that she is the newest generation in the battle for gender equity in collegiate athletics. And while the pace of progress has been increasing, Hurlbut is ever mindful of her responsibilities. Anyone breaking new ground must deal with the fact that, if they falter, they may ruin it for others coming through the ranks.

"You realize that you may be scrutinized a little more intensely than a male in your position," Hurlbut said. "You're perhaps even more careful about what you do and how you represent the conference."

Hurlbut hopes her appointment and tenure at the Patriot League will open some doors for other women breaking into the athletics profession. Hurlbut's optimism is not unfounded. While some institutions refuse to accept change and continue to waste resources in fruitless court cases, other institutions, conferences, and state governments are taking proactive measures to implement Title IX and gender equity. Two of the most ardent football conferences, the Big Ten and the Southeastern Conference (SEC), have taken league-wide measures to insist member institutions comply with Title IX.

In June 1992, the Big Ten Conference presidents agreed, unanimously, to achieve a 60/40 male/female participation ratio by June 30, 1997. Part two of the plan was to match the undergraduate population ratio by the year 2002, but that part of the plan did not get voted on. At the time of the vote, athletic participation in the Big Ten was 69.5 percent male.[42]

In June 1993, the SEC revealed that, beginning in the 1995–1996 academic year, each SEC school will be required to offer a minimum of two more women's sports than men's sports. To encourage emerging women's sports, the SEC will offer championships for any sport in which one-third of the league's schools are participating.[43]

In response to these conference mandates, some institutions have taken the plan further on their own campuses. Penn State, the Big Ten's newest member, announced a number of improvements in July 1993. Penn State reported that it will increase scholarships for female student-athletes, elevate women's soccer to varsity status, implement reasonable participation caps on men's sports, add a female team physician; award endowed athletic scholarships to women, increase funding in the sports promotions and marketing areas, encourage coaches of women's teams to attract the maximum number of team members, conduct an internal Title IX review, increase the scholarship level in volleyball to the full NCAA limit, review intramural and club sport activity to ensure interests are being met and encouraged, and, finally, identify, as an institution, additional enhancement opportunities.[44]

The University of Iowa also took the conference's initiative one step further. In April 1992, the University of Iowa Board in Control of Athletics unanimously passed a proposal to give female student-athletes access in proportion to their representation in the undergraduate student body within the next five years. Iowa's undergraduate enrollment, at the time of the decision, was 49 percent men to 51 percent women. In July 1993, the university increased the salary of women's basketball coach Vivian Stringer to match that of the men's coach, Dr. Tom Davis. The identical salaries are $117,872. The institution followed that up in September 1993, when it announced its decision to add crew as an intercollegiate sport in the fall of 1994.[45]

"Our institution took the Big Ten plan and said this is a great idea, but it's far too long a period of time to ask the women to wait. That is why we moved our plan up to equal within five years," said Dr. Grant. "We are going to attempt to do it without in any way diminishing the quality of our men's program."

In May 1995, the University of Maine released a plan to increase the budget for women's sports by $724,000 by 1997 in order to bring the school into compliance with the federal requirements. The increased funding, which will not result in cuts in the men's program, will come from a dedicated share of ticket sales from the Alfond Arena Sports Complex, donations, and income from endowments.[46]

In June 1993, the University of Denver announced plans to enhance their women's athletic program. The university will allocate $200,000 for new full-time and part-time coaches for women's sports, recruiting, scholarships, salaries, facilities, and operating and travel expenses budgeted for the 1993–1994 academic year. Specific plans at the Division II school included reallocating five scholarships to women's programs, appointing assistant coaches in volleyball and women's basketball, upgrading women's soccer and volleyball head coaches to full-time status, increasing funds for advertising and promoting women's sports, and increasing funds allocated to operating budgets.[47]

The Gulf South Conference, in September 1993, planned a league-wide gender equity policy. Seven conference schools would join the eighth, North Alabama, in compliance orders from the Office of Civil Rights. North Alabama was found in violation of Title IX, and this marked the first time a conference had based its equity efforts on a complaint filed against a member institution. The Gulf South is a Division II conference.

North Alabama's remedies included promises to recruit female athletes more actively, generate publicity for the women's programs, upgrade the women's schedules, and provide the women's teams with more money for travel, better equipment, and a fair share of the institution's practice and playing facilities.[48]

In the summer of 1995, the Louisiana State Legislature passed a bill that provides up to fifty tuition wavers per year for female student-athletes at each state-supported college or university. Intended to increase opportunities for women while aiding football-playing institutions in the move toward Title IX, the bill will also release $1 million for use by athletic departments in other areas. Gary Forster, sponsor of the bill, used the "football is in jeopardy" plea as the rallying cry. The bill passed 97–4 in the House and 33–0 in the Senate.[49]

The state governments in California (May 1993) and Florida (February 1993) passed bills to force the institutions, on all levels, to come into Title IX compliance. California's bill requires proportionality by 1998–1999, a report to the state legislature on progress, and, in that report by trustees, a description of the efforts being made and the extent to which compliance has been achieved.[50] This bill, while favorable in theory, displays another example of why institutions should take Title IX compliance into their own hands. This bill totally ignores the second and third prongs of the OCR compliance test.

Florida would penalize institutions not in compliance by withholding state funds and making schools ineligible for competitive state grants. The law called for each institution to develop its own gender equity plan, to address all items in Title IX. This bill added enforcement language to an existing bill, the Florida Educational Equity Act, which previously had no penalties attached for noncompliance.[51]

Private enterprise has even gotten involved in providing solutions. In November 1993, Wells Fargo, which has 612 banks in California, struck deals with twelve California colleges to support a variety of women's sports. Some of the deals were worth as much as $50,000. Women make up 50 percent of the bank's business, so it was also a smart business maneuver for Wells Fargo. According to experts, this deal was a first for women's inter-collegiate athletics.[52]

Some other solutions seem obvious, but haven't been highly touted. In August 1995, the NCAA released its budget figures for the 1995–1996 year. Operating revenue was stated at $220,650,000, an increase of more than $16 million over the previous year. More than $13 million is expected in revenues over expenditures. Division I institutions are to receive $108,250,000 in revenue-distribution funds, a 13.9 percent increase over 1994–1995. The national office expenses are expected to be around $26,698,000 or approximately 12.1 percent of operating revenue. What is the average percent of operating budget for a nonprofit entity? Television revenue accounts for 82 percent of the NCAA's general operating budget, $1.78 million from the deal with CBS Sports for the television contract for the NCAA men's basketball tournament, and $2.5 million from ESPN for the broadcast rights to the women's tournament. The only line item in the NCAA budget for gender equity is $30,000 earmarked for the Gender Equity Resource Center.[53]

There are a couple of issues here. As the governing body and supposed leader of intercollegiate athletics, perhaps the NCAA could take a stronger stand on the issue. Perhaps the NCAA could withhold revenue-sharing checks to institutions that are not in Title IX compliance. But that could damage its relationships with advertisers, television networks, bowl and tournament organizers, and so on, and thereby jeopardize their revenue. Perhaps the NCAA should set the example and slash its extravagant oper-ating budget and direct that money to institutions specifically for Title IX compliance plans.

If the college football and men's basketball coaches feel threatened by Title IX, maybe a deal could be worked out with the National Football League and the National Basketball Association whereby those two leagues would provide financial assistance to institutions. Realistically, the NCAA, whether or not it so desires, serves as a minor league feeder system for professional football and basketball. It only seems sensible that the professional leagues would want to help preserve their minor league affiliates.

5

Showtime

We need a blueprint. We need not be standing on opposite sides of the law, shooting bows and arrows at each other. There is a way to do it, if we all become part of the blueprint, part of the process to solve it. It has got to be done. We have got to put our egos aside.
                                    —Betty Jaynes, executive director,
                                    Women's Basketball Coaches Association

"See the ball," the coach implores the players as a defensive lapse is committed. The coach is standing now, constantly, never relenting, pacing the sideline as the team battles the opponent. The coach's height alone can intimidate, and when "the stare" is provoked by a questionable referee's call, no words need be spoken for the offender to receive the message. The coach continues to coax the players, chide the officials, and encourage the players. No official is safe from the coach's glare, and yet the demeanor changes, like Jekyll and Hyde, when it comes to the players. No. This is not John Thompson or Bobby Knight.

Theresa Grentz has one of the most successful coaching records in women's college basketball, and the former Rutgers mentor shows her diverse abilities this December night in 1993. Rutgers is hosting its annual Holiday Tournament, and the Lady Knights are hosting highly ranked Colorado, Atlantic 10 foe Rhode Island, and Drexel University. Another top-ranked team, Purdue, backed out of the tournament at the last minute and diluted the strength of the field, but the tourney moves on.

Grentz's young Mexican center, Gabriela Gonzalez, needs Grentz's support this night. Although she is 6 feet, 4 inches tall and possesses international experience from playing with the Mexican national team, Gonzalez's game is a little unrefined. She plays hard and will go on to make the all-tournament team at this event. But Grentz treads lightly. She understands the fragile psyche of the player and does not shout or holler. After a subtle sideline conference is conducted between free throws, the junior center is ready to return.

This used to be the Bell Atlantic Rutgers Holiday Tournament, but Bell Atlantic pulled out as the lead sponsor. According to Rutgers' associate athletic director for promotions, Kevin MacConnell, Bell felt, as a regional company, that its advertising dollars were tied up in a New Jersey–based event, and it felt that not many people knew that Bell is the parent company for New Jersey Bell, the Bell Yellowpages. Basically, the company felt that it wasn't getting its money's worth. It claimed that it wanted to do more regional advertising. MacConnell must find a replacement for Bell, and one wonders whether Bell would have pulled out had the tournament been a men's tournament.

On the floor, Grentz is back at it, giving a player two palms up and assuring the player, "It's all right, it's all right," after the player missed a layup and the subsequent offensive rebound. Certainly this is not Bobby Knight. With about four minutes left in the contest, the teams leave the floor during a time-out, and Rutgers receives a standing ovation. The Lady Knights have a comfortable lead, and the victory is at hand, but it has not been easy. There is not a lot of difference in talent between these two teams this night. The difference is Grentz.

Her team plays hard, intelligently, and with a good deal of poise. The most distinct characteristic, though, is the team's relentless effort. Determined and tenacious, the Lady Knights finally broke the spirit of the opponent. Highly ranked Colorado will pose a larger obstacle in the championship game the following evening, but this opening game has given Grentz and her players a solid springboard.

For those who have never experienced a women's collegiate basketball game, it is something worth witnessing. The atmosphere is completely different from the men's game. North Carolina's Charlotte Smith, in 1994, became the first woman since West Virginia's Georgeann Wells to dunk in a game (1984–1985), but that type of emphatic display is not a staple of the women's game. The women's game is what Dr. James Naismith envisioned when he propped up his first peach basket. The women's game is a team game. Without the threat of a two-handed, in-your-face tomahawk dunk, the women rely on the fundamentals of defense, passing, ball movement, and discipline. The great programs, like those at Tennessee, Stanford, Connecticut, and others have brought the women's game to new levels of interest, have buried the stereotypes of slow, boring action.

Between games at the Rutgers Holiday Tournament, Marian Washington, the head women's coach at the University of Kansas, and her assistant Renee Brown are in the crow's nest near the newspaper reporters. Their Jayhawks are participating in a tournament in New York City, just across the river from New Jersey, and the two women are taking detailed notes and conducting a rapid scouting report of Big Eight Conference foe Colorado. Business as usual.

Three months later, in the first week of March, Rutgers closes its regular season against conference opponent Saint Bonaventure. Lady Knights' senior Caroline DeRoose is honored before the game, and it is a special occasion for the team captain from Belgium. It will be hard for Grentz to replace her since she has led the team in scoring, free throw percentage, and minutes played. More important is her leadership on the floor. She is the Lady Knights' go-to player in clutch situations, and she rarely fails. This final regular season matchup prior to the Atlantic 10 tournament is really just an exercise for the Lady Knights.

The team has greatly improved since December, a kudo to Grentz who has just the one senior and a suspect bench. This will be the last year in a string of nine consecutive twenty-victory seasons and nine consecutive appearances in the NCAA tournament for Grentz's program. The team will also capture its second consecutive conference title. Along the way, Grentz and company will record a historical win. In mid-January, the number-one-ranked, unbeaten Tennessee Volunteers visited Rutgers, and the Lady Knights pulled off an 87–77 upset. Never before in the eighteen-year history of the Associated Press women's basketball poll had an unranked team beaten the number one team. DeRoose scored a career-high thirty-five points, including five-for-five from the three-point line and ten of eleven from the free throw line.

Grentz built a women's basketball stronghold at Rutgers University (before leaving New Brunswick for the new challenge of coaching in the Big Ten for the University of Illinois in the summer of 1995). In nineteen seasons on the bench guiding the Lady Knights' program, Grentz racked up more than 425 victories, six Atlantic 10 regular season titles, and four Atlantic 10 tournament championships.

She coached three All-Americans and one Player of the Year and has received numerous Coach of the Year honors. Her two greatest achievements were her 1982 Association of Intercollegiate Athletics for Women (AIAW) National Championship team and her selection as the head coach for the 1992 women's Olympic team. Lofty accomplishments for most, these are routine for this pioneer of women's basketball.

Grentz was a three-time All-American and once Player of the Year (1974) for tiny Immaculata College in the early 1970s, the first women's college basketball power. After her playing career, Grentz took a part-time head coaching job with Saint Joseph's and led the Hawks to a two-year mark of 27–5. In 1976, after a dismal season, Rutgers was searching for a new women's head coach. When Grentz was selected for the position, she became the first full-time women's basketball coach. During her tenure, she brought tremendous success and recognition to the Rutgers program, so much so that the Louis Brown Athletic Center hosted the 1993–1994 NCAA East Regional for the NCAA tournament.

Eventual national champion North Carolina, the University of Connecticut, Vanderbilt University, and Southern Mississippi put on an incredible display of basketball for two days. Thanks to Grentz, women's basketball fans in the New York–New Jersey metropolitan area saw some of the country's best players and best coaches in the 1993–1994 season. Some of the best fans of the women's game also visited the New Brunswick campus. Enthusiasts cheering for UConn during the regionals conveyed the message that Huskymania is not strictly reserved for the men's team. That is indicative of the immense growth and enthusiasm the women's game has experienced over the last five years.

"Finesse basketball is a key ingredient in the women's game, especially since our game is played below the rim," said Betty Jaynes, executive director of the Women's Basketball Coaches Association. "Women's basketball requires masterful strategy by its coaches. The women's game is more of a coaches' game since the power element is not as prominent as it is in the men's game. This is not to say that coaching is less significant in men's basketball, but rather women's coaches must also compensate for the challenge of playing below the rim.

"The dunk would definitely add a new dynamic to women's basketball if it becomes commonplace over the next five years," Jaynes continued. "However, the women's game has progressed extremely well over the last two decades without the dunk, and will continue to do so with the growing acceptance of females participating in sport. Yet, the dunk will attract those basketball fans who are now acclimated to the power element of the men's game."

According to a 1994 survey conducted by the American Basketball

Council, more than 13.5 million females, ages six to fifty-five, were participating in basketball—an increase of 23 percent since 1987. Basketball is the top team sport for female participants. This trend is reflected in fan attendance at women's college games during the same time span. For four consecutive seasons, from 1992–1993 to 1995–1996, the women's Final Four has been sold out well in advance. During the last three of those years, the event has been sold out a year in advance.

Tennessee drew more than 15,000 on two occasions in the 1993–1994 season, while Rutgers averaged more than 2,000 fans during the same season. Since the mid–1980s, the Rutgers women's team has frequently outdrawn the men's team, as have other women's programs, including Tennessee.

The University of Iowa, a leader in women's athletics, noticed this attendance trend in 1992–1993 and sponsored the Women's Basketball Attendance Challenge for the 1993–1994 season. The top ten teams in attendance from the previous year (UConn, Southwest Missouri State, Ohio State, Tennessee, Texas, Iowa, Stanford, Vanderbilt, Texas Tech, and Virginia) were invited to compete. The savvy marketing scheme paid off because all ten participants experienced attendance increases. Tennessee had the largest increase of more than 4,000 per game for an average attendance of almost 11,000 fans. Ohio State and Texas experienced similar increases.[1] Texas women's basketball remains one of the top attendance draws *of any sport* in the Southwest Conference. Thompson-Boling Arena in Knoxville holds the world record for attendance at a women's basketball game when it packed 24,563 fans in for a December 1987 contest against the University of Texas.

"I think it was our challenge early on, and I think the thing we wanted to disprove was women's athletics, women's basketball in particular, could not be a spectator sport," said Texas head coach Jody Conradt. "We had as our primary goal to put people in the stands, sell season tickets, and to promote women's basketball. It would always be compared to men's basketball, there is no way to get around that. But at the same time we sell it with its own uniqueness and its own ability to generate excitement and enthusiasm.

"We did a grass roots campaign," Conradt went on. "We believed if you could get them to the game once, they would come back. I think in a lot of ways programs around the country have modeled what happened here at Texas. Once we started to post some numbers, it became apparent to people that there was potential. A few programs across the country showed that it could be done and those programs also put pressure on other teams in their conference and across the country. I don't care what sport you play at the collegiate level, nobody likes to get hammered all the time. The competition eventually forces people to speed up their time table."

According to NCAA statistics for the 1994–1995 season, almost 5 million fans attended women's college basketball games, a 9 percent increase over the previous year and the fourteenth consecutive year attendance has increased. The Big Ten Conference averaged more than 3,000 fans per women's home basketball games, a national record, buoyed by Ohio State, Iowa, Penn State, Purdue, and Wisconsin, each of whom averaged more than 4,000 fans per home event. Until 1994–1995, no conference had averaged 3,000 fans per game, but in this season, the Big Ten was joined by the Southwest Conference with an average of 3,042 per contest.[2]

The NCAA also noticed this significant rise in popularity and increased the Women's Basketball Championships field from forty-eight to sixty-four for the 1993–1994 tournament. According to the NCAA, more than 250,000 people attended women's tournament games that season.[3] The organization was rewarded again in the 1994–1995 Final Four in Minneapolis, when the 17,328-seat Target Center was sold out for the two-day event. The 1996 tournament held at the 22,949-seat Charlotte Coliseum was the earliest women's Final Four sellout of all time.

The media have also taken notice. The women's game was rewarded in December 1994 when ESPN purchased the television rights to nineteen NCAA championships, including exclusive rights to all rounds of the women's NCAA tournament. Beginning with the 1996 tournament, ESPN will televise, live, twenty-three games of the tournament, giving the tournament exposure it has never before realized. Of the twenty-three games to be broadcast, only three will be televised at the same time as men's games, so the women will have little competition for visibility. And the women will finally get the day off they wanted.

In the men's Final Four, the teams receive a day off between the semifinals and the championship game. Until the new ESPN deal, the women had to play the semifinals and the championship game on consecutive days. The former television network for the women's tourney, CBS Sports, forced the scheduling. If the women wanted to be on national television, it could not compete with the men's game, so the compromise was an early Saturday tip-off for the semifinals for the women followed by a Sunday championship game, while the men played prime time on Saturday and Monday night. In a Friday-Sunday format, ESPN's deal guarantees the women their day of rest.

It was also a smart buy for ESPN. The all-sports network saw its women's semifinals in 1994–1995 draw a 1.4 rating, and its four tournament games averaged a 1.1 rating (approximately 700,000 households). Executives compared that to the station's National Hockey League average of 1.0. The national championship game between Tennessee and UConn drew a 5.7 rating and a 15 point share, the highest rated women's championship this decade.[4]

"There is no question that the market value has changed and grown tremendously," said Tennessee coach Pat Summitt. "I think the awareness level today as compared to ten years ago . . . I think people who understand basketball appreciate the women's game. It is a game played with the execution of fundamentals. Team play is critical in women's basketball because we don't have the great one-on-one players that can overpower a game. But I think we have a game that basketball-educated people really enjoy. I think the television exposure has also served as a real positive."

Anyone still needing convincing of the popularity of women's basketball need only look as far as Storrs, Connecticut. The Huskies completed a storybook season with a 70–64 victory over Tennessee in the 1995 championship game to finish with a 35–0 record, the best record in the history of college basketball for men or women. Coach Geno Auriemma and his team were mobbed by thousands of fans at the airport after their arrival home from their Final Four conquest. More than 9,000 fans crammed Gampel Pavilion for a pep rally to honor the team, and an estimated 100,000 Huskymaniacs attended a state capitol parade to recognize the team's achievement.

To further cement its growing popularity and to document the tradition, history, and struggles of women's basketball, construction for the Women's Basketball Hall of Fame was scheduled to begin in July 1995. The hall, located in Jackson, Tennessee, will be funded by a variety of sources, primarily the annual preseason State Farm Hall of Fame Classic, featuring the top four teams in the women's preseason poll.

Why has women's basketball become the flagship for women's athletics? Why has women's basketball achieved such high interest and earned the commitment of television contracts? The reasons are many, but the foundation began with and continues with a handful of coaches who have not only championed the cause of their own team, but have promoted women's basketball and women's athletics as well. These coaches have developed marketing strategies, have implemented promotional campaigns, and have grasped every opportunity to speak up for their sport. While building their own programs from the ground up, they have also kept an eye on the bigger picture and tossed a few bricks into the cornerstone of the sport for which they hold tremendous passion.

Not many women would be questioned about coaching a men's collegiate basketball team. It just isn't done; it just hasn't been done. Who could even think of such a ridiculous idea? The people in Knoxville, Tennessee, have. When the fortunes of the men's basketball program at the University of Tennessee were not very bright a few years ago, Pat Summitt was asked, by the Knoxville media, if she would ever consider coaching the men's team. Summitt, with the diplomacy of a sincere politician, sidestepped the inquiries. Could Summitt undertake the task? Absolutely no question about it.

Pat Summitt is a coaching legend—men's basketball, women's basketball, Catholic Youth Organization (CYO), playground league, any league. Borrowing a phrase from ESPN commentator Dick Vitale, Summitt can flat out coach basketball.

In twenty-one years at the helm of Tennessee's Lady Volunteers basketball program, Summitt has achieved standards to be envied by anyone who desires to be the best. Her teams have won more than 530 games to make her the second most successful coach in terms of games won in women's basketball history. In twelve of the previous nineteen seasons entering the 1995–1996 campaign, the Lady Vols had advanced to the Final Four and had completed nineteen consecutive seasons of at least twenty victories. Summitt guided her team to the national championship three times, in 1987, 1989, and 1991, and four times the Lady Vols have finished second.

Summitt's regular season winning percentage is more than 81 percent, and her postseason mark is higher than 77 percent. Entering the 1995–1996 campaign, the Lady Vols had appeared in all fourteen NCAA women's basketball tournaments, and no team has won more games in the history of the women's NCAA tournament. It's no wonder Thompson-Boling Arena is the biggest draw in women's basketball. Up to 1995–1996, Summitt's teams had captured seven Southeastern Conference (SEC) regular season titles and six SEC tournament championships.

Summitt also has a 63–4 international record and was the head coach when the United States brought home the first ever women's basketball gold medal from the 1984 Olympics. As a collegiate player, Summitt herself won a silver medal with the women's team at the 1976 Olympic games.

Equally impressive is Summitt's 100 percent graduation rate, and the twenty-two players who have earned Academic All-SEC, an average of one per Summitt's twenty-one seasons.

If Pat Summitt is a legend, then Jody Conradt is a Hall of Famer. The head coach of the Texas Lady Longhorns, Conradt has many coaching records her counterparts are chasing. She is the winningest all-time coach in women's basketball with more than 650 victories. On a list of the winningest all-time men's coaches, by percentage, Conradt ranks fifth (.798), behind John Wooden and Adolph Rupp. On the winningest active coaches list, by victories, Conradt ranks fourth behind Dean Smith, James Phelan, and Don Haskins, yet ahead of notables such as Lefty Driesell and Bob Knight. On the all-time winningest coaches list, by victories, Conradt is tenth, again ahead of Knight, Driesell, and Jerry Tarkanian.

During a twelve-year stretch from 1978 to 1990, Conradt's Lady Longhorns won 183 consecutive games against Southwest Conference (SWC) opponents. Entering the 1994–1995 season, Conradt's team had always won at least twenty games and had always been invited to postseason competition. Until Connecticut duplicated the feat in 1994–1995, the 1986 Texas women's team was the only one to finish its season unbeaten (34–0), capturing Conradt's one national championship in the process.

When she entered her twentieth season at Austin in 1995–1996, Conradt's teams had been ranked in the final Associated Press Top 20 poll fourteen consecutive seasons, including four straight at number one (1983–1987). Conradt has collected the national coach of the year award three times, Southwest Conference coaching honors four times, and numerous other accolades. She has coached nineteen All Americans and two Players of the Year. In the thirteen-year history of women's basketball in the SWC, Texas has won the regular season title nine times and captured the tournament championship nine times as well, with two second-place finishes.

The significant elements here are that these coaches have not only built successful basketball programs, but also have developed the programs beyond the court of play and have created models for others to emulate. These coaches, and their players, do more than devise game plans. They have become involved in their communities and fortified not only the athletic departments of which they are members, but the institutions they represent.

At Texas, for example, the Longhorn Associates (for Excellence in Women's Athletics) is a support organization specifically for the women's athletic program at Texas. Donors can invest anywhere from $55 to $10,000 (or more) annually in the women's athletic program. A donor's gift can be utilized to endow scholarships for Lady Longhorn student-athletes, or the gift may be unrestricted, which enables the UT athletic department to utilize the donation where it is needed, whether that is to support the Dana X. Bible Academic Center for Longhorn student-athletes or to enhance the physical facilities for which Texas has become known.

The development of this organization was not only intelligent, it was vital to the program. Texas state law prohibits the use of tax dollars to support athletics programs, so private support is necessary. Additionally, the university is required, under state law, to charge its athletic programs for the use of university facilities, such as the Frank Erwin Center where the men's and women's basketball teams compete.

Longhorn Associates are also asked to be participants in the Lady Longhorns program, and, as part of their gift to the organization, are entitled to seating and parking for athletic contests, educational seminars at the university, lunch with the coaches, and other tokens of appreciation.

Lady Longhorn players are also more than students and athletes. Through a four-year-old program, called Neighborhood Longhorns, student-athletes attempt to provide a positive influence to the lives of Austin's at-risk youth. The program is designed for Texas student-athletes to support these youth in their social and academic endeavors by providing positive role models, encouragement, and support. Longhorn student-athletes visit youngsters in recreational facilities and housing projects to deliver their positive message. Sponsors also reward children who participate in the program and do well academically with savings bonds for college. Lady Longhorns also volunteer their time to speak to children at elementary schools, visit elderly Longhorn fans in nursing homes, or brighten the day of a child in a local children's hospital.

Similarly at Tennessee, about six years ago, a campaign called the Winners' Circle Scholarships was started. This long-range effort was established by the women's athletic program to create fully funded, endowed scholarships for the entire Lady Vols basketball program in order to ensure that female student-athletes would always be able to earn a college degree and compete for the university. Entering the 1994–1995 season, ten scholarships were endowed or pledged to be endowed at the $100,000 level. In addition to the basketball scholarships, pledges have been made for other women's programs including golf, softball, swimming and diving, tennis, track and field, volleyball, and general awards as well.

Women's basketball programs at Tennessee, Rutgers, and Texas have also initiated youth groups in order to interest elementary school and junior high school girls in women's basketball. The Little Lady Knights club at Rutgers has more than 100 girls involved in the program, and these participants are invited to certain Lady Knights' home games where they get to meet the players and are able to experience the thrills of college basketball.

The University of Connecticut developed strategic plans to maximize the success of its team in 1995. The athletic department promoted players to national talk shows, and Rebecca Lobo appeared on "CBS This Morning" and the "Late Show with David Letterman." The university cooperated with the *Hartford Courant* to produce a 144-page book on the Huskies' season. The book, called *UConn 35–0: The Championship Season*, sold more than 10,000 copies. The university also produced a sixty-minute video highlighting the season.

The athletic department also created a collector's card to commemorate the occasion.[5] Finally, in July 1995, the university announced a three-year television contract with Connecticut Public Television. Although other teams in the athletic program will receive exposure, the deal was struck primarily for fans of the Huskies' women's basketball team. Over the three years of the deal, CPTV will broadcast live fifty-one women's basketball games (seventeen per season). CPTV will also air a dozen coach's shows with head coach Geno Auriemma. With other programming and marketing projects, the deal is expected to net the university nearly $1.5 million over the life of the contract.[6]

While Summitt and Conradt are two of the all-time ambassadors of women's basketball, it would be remiss to overlook others who have made similar efforts, including Vivian Stringer at Rutgers, Leon Barmore at Louisiana Tech, Tara VanDerveer at Stanford, Debbie Ryan at Virginia, Rene Portland at Penn State, Marian Washington at Kansas, Jim Foster at Vanderbilt, and Andy Landers at Georgia, among others. Despite the monumental efforts and longtime vigilance of these coaches, however, all is still not well with the marquee women's sport.

Marianne Stanley probably watched with anger, resentment, disappointment, and sadness as "her" University of Southern California Trojans lost to Louisiana Tech, 75–66, in the Mideast Regional championship of the 1993–1994 women's NCAA basketball tournament. Stanley may have felt some vindication as well. Stanley took over the USC women's basketball program in 1989 and rebuilt it to the level of excellence it had enjoyed in the early 1980s. With three-time All-American Lisa Leslie, Stanley's 1993–1994 squad was her best and was picked by prognosticators as one of the favorites to challenge for the national championship. But, after having recruited the players, coached them, taught them, done all those things asked of a Division I basketball coach at a premier Division I institution, Stanley was not permitted to see her project to completion. Instead of doing what she loves to do more than anything else, Marianne Stanley is embroiled in a highly publicized, highly controversial lawsuit against her former employer.

Stanley's initial contract was a four-year deal worth $60,000 per year that was increased in 1992 to $62,000. Anticipating the conclusion of the contract in June 1993, Stanley initiated negotiations with the Trojan athletic director, Mike Garrett, the previous April, with the hope that the contract would be finalized before the conclusion of the existing deal. Stanley indicated to Garrett that she wanted a contract equal to that of USC men's coach George Raveling. Raveling, at the time, was reported to be making a base salary in the neighborhood of $130,000. Garrett responded with a three-year contract proposal with base salaries of $86,000 in the first year, $96,000 in the second year, and $106,000 in the third year. This offer was verified by Garrett in writing. Stanley spurned the offer.

Approximately one month later, on June 7, Stanley and Garrett met to discuss the contract proposals, and Garrett again offered the same three-year deal he originally initiated. Stanley countered with a three-year deal that paid her $96,000 the first half of the contract and then matched Raveling's for the second eighteen months of the agreement. Garrett dismissed that proposition.

In mid-June, after Garrett failed to answer several inquiries, Stanley sought the assistance of Timothy Stoner, a Philadelphia lawyer and the legal counsel for the Women's Basketball Coaches Association. Stoner attempted to intervene on Stanley's behalf and negotiate her contract with Garrett.

Stoner proposed to Garrett, over the telephone, a three-year contract with an automatic two-year renewal clause and base salaries of $88,000, $97,000, and $112,000. Stoner proposed incentives, as well, such as room and board for Stanley's daughter, who was planning to attend USC in the fall of 1993, radio and television shows that would highlight Stanley and the USC women's program, and monetary bonuses for achievements such as conference championships, NCAA victories, and coach of the year awards. Stoner also indicated that Stanley would accept more salary and fewer incentives or vice versa.

Garrett again disapproved and withdrew his three-year offer. Instead, he issued Stoner his final offer—a one-year contract with a base salary of $96,000 with no renewal clause and a stipulation that Stanley would forever waive her right to sue the institution.

On July 13, Stanley again requested the three-year contract with the incentive package. Garrett responded that USC's offer was the one-year deal at $96,000, and he told Stanley that she had just twenty-four hours to respond. The following day, Stanley sent a memorandum to Garrett asking for more time to consider the offer, since she was distressed by Garrett's withdrawal of the three-year offer.

On July 15, Garrett informed Stanley that, since she had not responded to his offer by the required deadline, his offer was no longer on the table. He indicated he would listen to any proposals Stanley might have, but he also indicated he was initiating the search process to fill Stanley's position, since her contract had run out and she had not signed a new one.

On August 5, 1993, Stanley filed an $8 million lawsuit against the University of Southern California and Mike Garrett. Stanley alleges Garrett withdrew the multiyear offer in retaliation for Stanley's demand to be compensated at the same level as Raveling. Stanley's sex discrimination lawsuit alleges violations of the Equal Pay Act, Title IX, the California constitution, and the Fair Employment and Housing Act, as well as retaliation, wrongful discharge in violation of public policy, breach of implied-in-fact employment contract, intentional infliction of emotional distress, and conspiracy. Stanley also filed for an injunction that would allow her to continue to coach until her case could be decided on its merits by a jury. The Federal Pay Act requires equal pay for positions that require equal skill, effort, and responsibility and are performed under similar working conditions. According to Stanley, when she took over the program in 1989, USC indicated its expectations were for Stanley to produce a winning program, and if she accomplished that objective, she would be adequately compensated for her endeavor.

"I don't think the university dealt in good faith with coach Stanley from the outset," said Stoner. "Both sides originally agreed to wait until a decision was rendered by the court. But when coach Stanley's injunction was dismissed by the judge, the school had the right to hire Cheryl Miller. The judge in this case went off on a Title VII tangent, stating that equity is not to be used to make a person whole. The judge missed the point. The problem is we don't have enough case law to support Title IX."

Many would question why Stanley failed to accept any of Garrett's offers, because they were more than generous (for a woman) and many would gladly accept such a compensation package. The question is not whether Stanley should have accepted any of the contract proposals. The question is whether Stanley was treated fairly and equitably. Were her demands to be compensated the same as Raveling outrageous? Did she deserve the compensation she was requesting? Did Stanley perform her duties, as outlined by the university, to the best of her abilities, and to a high level of success?

Stanley's coaching resumé is superior to Raveling's. Raveling's overall winning percentage during his twenty-two seasons is slightly above .500 with no national championships to his credit. During his tenure at USC, he was under .500 (99–106) entering the 1993–1994 season with just three postseason appearances for the Trojans; the most successful trip was a quarterfinal appearance in the National Invitational Tournament (NIT), unquestionably an inferior commodity in comparison to the NCAA tournament.

During Stanley's seventeen years as a head coach, she guided teams to four national championships, including three at Old Dominion where she achieved a winning percentage of more than 81 percent in her ten years as the Monarchs' coach. She earned numerous coach of the year awards and coached U.S. teams in international competition as well. At USC, she guided the Trojans to four NCAA tournament appearances in five seasons, taking her team to the Sweet 16 two consecutive years prior to her dismissal. She earned the PAC-10 Coach of the Year award in 1993.[7] At the time, the only credential Raveling had over Stanley was four more years in the business, and not very productive ones at that. Not only did Stanley perform the same duties as Raveling, but she accomplished those requirements to a much greater degree of success.

Attorneys for USC, as well as the judges that denied Stanley's requests for injunctions, have stated that the USC men's basketball program and the USC women's basketball program are different. These legal experts have stated the coaching jobs for both of these programs are different in level of responsibility, stature, and revenue production. Judges at every phase of appeal have prevented witnesses to support Stanley's case from testifying. While it noted that a trial had yet to be held, the qualitative differences in the men's and women's programs justified a different level of pay. The court also stated that revenue generation is an important factor that can be considered in justifying pay discrepancies, and the amount of revenue generated should be considered in determining whether responsibilities and working conditions are substantially equal. The court also stated that Raveling's qualifications and experience were substantially different, and the employer can consider marketplace value of an individual's skills in determining compensation.

The question is not whether the men's basketball team attracts more fans, makes more money, or generates more publicity (and it is hard to believe that a national championship–caliber team with a three-time All-American and Player of the Year candidate would not generate more positive publicity for the university than the mediocre men's team). Those intangibles are not written, at least not until this case, into coaching contracts.

In a *New York Times* article, the defense attorney for USC stated that the reason Stanley's request for a salary equal to Raveling's was rejected is that the men's and women's basketball programs at USC are different.[8] Was the university inadvertently admitting it was treating its basketball programs inequitably?

"Under Title IX, you cannot distinguish base salaries on the basis that one program is revenue-generating and one is not," explained Stoner. "Under the Equal Pay Act, if the jobs are substantially the same, they are working for the same employer under the same conditions and circumstances, exhibiting the same skills, you cannot justify paying the women's coach less [in base salary]. You must look at the credentials for the job.

"If a women's coach has not been given the opportunity to coach a revenue-producing sport, that cannot be used as justification for paying her less than the men's coach."

Is Marianne Stanley's job description the same as George Raveling's? Did they both administer their programs, recruit players, oversee personnel, arrange Top 25 schedules, and perform all the other ancillary activities of a head basketball coach? If the answer is yes, then Stanley deserves the same base salary as the men's coach, regardless of who it is. If the two coaches in question have the same education, skill, experience, and duties under similar working conditions, the base salary should be the same.

In regard to USC's and the court's claims that revenue generation, fan support, and publicity are viable factors for the disparity in salary, if USC has, as most universities have historically done, underfunded its women's programs, and Stanley has not, due to the lack of resources and support, had an opportunity to generate revenue, increase fan support, or publicity, how can she be held accountable for a task she was not expected to perform and was not supported sufficiently to accomplish? The other significant point missed in this whole scenario is that the USC women's team members also had a legitimate Title IX lawsuit to pursue. One of the fundamental principals of Title IX, in regard to coaching, deals specifically with the quality of coaching accorded to a women's team.

The players of the women's team are entitled to a coach possessing similar credentials to the coach of the opposite men's team. In this case, USC pulled a publicity stunt by hiring former Trojan star Cheryl Miller to take Stanley's place. While Miller is arguably the best women's basketball player of the modern era, her coaching credentials do not stack up. Prior to taking the

USC job, Miller had never had any head coaching experience on any level—not college, high school, or recreation league. She had a brief stint as an assistant, but she spent most of that time moonlighting as a television commentator. Whether you compare Miller's coaching resumé to either Raveling's or Stanley's, it was no comparison. And the lack of experience was evident in the Trojan's aforementioned loss to Louisiana Tech when Miller was schooled by Lady Techster coach Leon Barmore. The Trojans team was denied quality coaching.

If Garrett had had the best interests of the institution and the women's basketball program at heart, he would have found a way to keep Stanley roaming the sidelines for that season. Garrett's actions caused a championship caliber team to carry emotional baggage and media scrutiny with it on every road trip that season. Instead of concentrating on winning the national championship, Leslie and her teammates spent their time trying to understand why their institution's athletic department had destroyed the program Stanley and the players helped build. It's difficult for soldiers to win the war when their own chiefs of staff are sabotaging the efforts.

As for Miller, after two tumultuous seasons, she resigned in the fall of 1995 to become a National Basketball Association reporter for Turner Sports. Raveling also retired from coaching prior to the 1994–1995 season due in part to complications and stress resulting from a car accident in the summer of 1994.

Ironically, around the same time Stanley was receiving defeat at every legal turn, her counterpart at Howard University, Sanya Tyler, was winning her Title IX lawsuit in a landmark case. In winning her case, Tyler became the first individual to be awarded monetary damages. A U.S. Superior Court jury awarded Tyler $2.39 million for Equal Pay Act, Title IX, and D.C. Human Rights Act violations. The judge later reduced the amount awarded to $1.1 million, and the university appealed the decision.

When Butch Beard was hired to coach the Howard men's program in 1990, he was given a salary of $78,000, a decent budget, and a car. Tyler had been with the university since 1980 and had guided her teams to six Mideastern Athletic Conference championships between 1982 and 1990. Her salary was $44,000, just over half of Beard's, and she claimed she had inferior locker room facilities and office space and no full-time assistant coach or secretary. Beard, like Cheryl Miller, had had no head coaching experience before taking the job at Howard. What Beard had was a solid resumé as a former NBA player.

Stoner was also involved, at the outset, with the case at Howard before he turned the case over to a counterpart in Washington, D.C. According to Stoner, before Howard hired Beard, Tyler was earning approximately $60,000 and performing two full-time jobs: women's basketball coach and senior women's administrator. When Howard hired Beard, the university wanted Tyler to take a pay cut to $40,000 but still perform her two jobs, while Beard would concentrate exclusively on men's basketball. In retrospect, Stoner would like to go back to Howard and tell them that for $20,000, this whole situation could have been avoided. Tyler just didn't want to, nor should she have been expected to, accept her salary being dropped by $20,000. Instead of paying Tyler what she deserved, Howard is out millions instead of $20,000.

Unfortunately, the university will not be penalized nearly as much as originally thought. In late September 1995, a trial court reduced Tyler's judgment even further—to $250,000—concluding the jury verdict was excessive against the university. The court also stated that the men's basketball coach had substantially more experience, skill, and knowledge of basketball than did Tyler and that there was more pressure on the men's coach than on Tyler to generate revenue and to win games.[9]

"The dilemma is lawyers representing universities either don't know, are not knowledgeable about Title IX, or choose to act in disregard of the law," Stoner said. "Lawyers rubber-stamp whatever their athletic directors want them to do. There are no checks and balances. We are going to see more and more lawsuits in the '90s. You can't balance the budget of athletic departments on the backs of women athletes and coaches. We are sending notice, that under the federal law, you cannot look at men's and women's coaches as two different jobs."

This disparity in coaching salaries, however, is not uncommon between men's and women's basketball, and in some other sports. Women's coaches in other sports have been successful in lawsuits as well. But the dilemma in women's college basketball is unique. Unlike their male counterparts, very few women's coaches have written, multiyear contracts. After the 1992–1993 season, at least twenty-five coaches of women's college basketball teams were fired or forced to resign. And the Stanley case has frightened away other potential litigants who fear losing their jobs if they stand up for their perceived rights.

"I think the Stanley case is a difficult situation," said Conradt. "I have been—and for a lack of a better word, amused is not a good one—interested in what's happened in terms of salary increases and trends in all of women's sports. We look at our Olympic sports, which is what we term them, and the men's and women's salaries have been comparable for some time. Then we start to see differences in the basketball programs and the salaries there.

"The rationale for that has always been the difference is dictated by marketplace," Conradt continued. "I think that is a hard argument to fight against. Obviously, the University of Texas could attract a women's basketball coach for significantly less than the men's program could. But again, it has to do with, do you want to go after the best. And how many of those are there out there in that elite class who have the credentials and the reputation that a university like Texas would seek out if they had an opening in the basketball program? All of this is pretty muddled in my mind, and we would like to see some clarity. Maybe it will have to come through lawsuits like the ones we see and will continue to see. I think everybody is holding their breath for a variety of reasons to see what is going to happen."

Important points of distinction must be made. Women's coaches are not asking for equal pay when the circumstances are not equal. A first-year women's coach, for example, could not require a salary equal to a men's coach who had been at the university for ten years and had achieved a certain degree of personal and team success. Even if tenure were equal, other factors should be weighed, such as educational preparation, experience, success (both in conference and postseason competition), graduation rates of student athletes, rankings, and public relations contributions.

What women's coaches are saying is that where all things are equal, the base salary should be equal. Additional compensation, in the form of bonuses, incentives, or endorsement packages, could be provided to the men's or women's coach for such things as high attendance figures, stellar fund-raising contributions, or national championships.

It's even more difficult to get any respect when male coaches of men's programs provide little support. In an ironic article appearing in the *Sunday Home News*, a central New Jersey daily newspaper, in February 1994, this issue was analyzed by comparing Theresa Grentz and men's coach Bob Wenzel. Wenzel had been with Rutgers for six years (when the story was done) and had a record of 90–81 at the time. He was making, according to public records, $132,930; Grentz was earning $103,200. Grentz's record has been stated and stands for itself. Wenzel, while leading the Scarlet Knights to four postseason appearances (two NCAA) had not won any Atlantic 10 conference championships or recorded any twenty-victory campaigns. Wenzel did a diplomatic two-step around the issue, but he did say it was like comparing apples and oranges because his and Grentz's jobs were different. The irony comes in when, in the summer of 1995, Vivian Stringer was hired to replace Grentz (who took the head coaching position at Illinois). Stringer is the fourth all-time winningest coach in women's college basketball with more than 500 career victories. To lure her away from the

University of Iowa, Rutgers made Stringer the highest paid women's basketball coach of all time with an annual minimum salary of $150,000, which could reach $300,000. Wenzel's salary, at the time, was $124,000.[10]

"This is such a complex question, and frankly I have mixed feelings about several aspects of it," said Iowa women's athletic director Dr. Christine Grant. "One of my biggest reservations is when some coaches, with their entire package, bring in twice as much as the university president or the governor of the state . . . I have a bit of a problem with that. We have a gender equity committee on campus and a subcommittee of that group that examines salaries.

"We started with the two basketball coaches because we thought that would be our biggest problem," Dr. Grant continued. "We had each coach submit a resumé, and we have a job description and we went through their qualifications. The one big difference was that the men's team brings in all these people and the women's team only brings in half that amount. The question was, is that a significant difference to warrant changes in compensation? Someone said, 'You know if Vivian Stringer was the coach of our men's team and Tom Davis was the coach of our women's team, the arena would still be filled for our men's team.' Having that said, we said we don't think that [attendance] is sufficient reason on our campus to warrant real differences in salaries."

The Women's Basketball Coaches Association conducted a salary survey in 1993, and there were a number of disappointing conclusions. The 246 Division I women's basketball coaches were polled, and 128 responded. According to the survey, head coaches of women's basketball teams earn an average base salary of $44,961, or just 59 percent of their male counterpart's average of $76,566. More than 73 percent of head coaches of men's teams make in excess of $60,000; only 27 percent of head coaches of women's teams make more than $60,000.

The most frequently cited salary range for head coaches of women's basketball was from $30,000 to $39,000; the most frequently cited salary range for men's head coaches was from $60,000 to $69,000. The highest salary range indicated for men's coaches was more than $200,000 whereas the highest range for women was from $130,000 to $139,000.

Additionally, the survey found that 92 percent of men's basketball coaches had contracts, and only 75 percent of women did. Of those women's coaches who do have contracts, 76 percent have contracts for three years or less in duration. Forty-one percent of men's coaches have contracts of four years or more, and 28 percent held contracts in the "other" category. Only 20 percent of head coaches of women's teams had rollover terms in their contracts, but 34 percent of their male counterparts did. Sadly, of the four teams in the women's 1994 Final Four, Alabama's Rick Moody, North Carolina's Sylvia Hatchell, and Purdue's Lin Dunn did not have written contracts. Only Louisiana Tech coach Leon Barmore had a written agreement.

Finally, the survey examined operating, travel, and recruiting budgets: the overall budgets for women's basketball programs averaged $148,194, whereas the budgets for men's programs averaged $252,922—a difference of $104,728. Another final question remains. Do women's coaches and female student-athletes want to fall into the same pitfalls that have haunted men's athletics over the years?

"We are being forced into a male model of sport that I always have had difficulty with philosophically," concluded Dr. Grant. "The question goes back to, is generating revenue a meritorious item that should be considered in such things? Athletics should be there for the kids to participate in an athletic endeavor they enjoy while they are getting their education. The imbalance is being created because of the fact there is so much money available in television, tournaments, and bowl games. That's where the imbalance comes in and the participation aspect has been deemphasized."

6

Basketball Nomads

> It is harder for a collegiate female player to play overseas than it is for a male player to make it to the NBA.
>
> —Jill Jeffrey, sports agent,
> Bruce Levy Associates

Had Carol Blazejowski been born ten years later, she would have been able to parlay her incredible basketball talents into a six-figure salary in a professional women's league—overseas. Blazejowski, or "Blaze," as she was known in her playing days, is a basketball Hall of Famer, enshrined in 1994. She holds some college basketball records that might never be broken. Unfortunately for Blazejowski, her date of birth limited her achievements to a boycotted Olympics in 1980 and a one-year stint in the defunct Women's Basketball League (WBL).

Blazejowski is director of women's basketball programs for the National Basketball Association (NBA), and she has been with the organization for more than five years. Ironically, the person who decides which sporting goods companies and gifts can bear the NBA logo had limited choices when her storied collegiate career came to a close. A three-time All-American at tiny Montclair State College, Blazejowski scored 3,199 points in her career, the most by a collegiate female and fourth all-time overall behind Pete Maravich, Freeman Williams, and Lionel Simmons.[1]

Her one-year season average of 38.6 in 1978 and career scoring average of 31.7 are women's basketball records, and she holds the single-game scoring mark for either gender in a storied Madison Square Garden game when she scored 52 points against Queens College in 1977.[2] She was the winner of the first Wade Trophy, the equivalent of football's Heisman Trophy, signifying the best player in women's collegiate basketball. She was the first athlete ever to have her uniform number (12) retired at Montclair State.[3]

Despite leading the nation in scoring in 1977 and 1978, and leading Montclair State, a nonscholarship institution, into the Final Four against the likes of UCLA, no professional teams anticipated drafting the five foot, eleven inch scoring machine. No sneaker companies offered lucrative endorsement deals. She won silver medals on World University and Pan American Games teams and gold medals playing in the Jones Cup, the World University Games, and the World Championships. She was elected captain for the 1980 Olympic team, but former president Jimmy Carter decided to boycott the Moscow games when Russia invaded Afghanistan. Blazejowski averaged thirty points per game in thirty-six WBL contests for the New Jersey Gems before the league folded in 1981, limiting the salary Blazejowski was able to draw from her three-year, $150,000 contract.[4]

"It's not so much frustration," said Blazejowski about her professional career that never had a chance. "It does cross my mind, especially when I see an NBA player whine about a ten-year, $100 million contract. I say 'wow' and I say he is lucky to be playing professional ball and getting paid for it.

"Don't I wish I could get just a piece of that. But it doesn't frustrate me. . . . I think about it and then it's gone because you have to live with what is. Hopefully things will get better and hopefully I have paved the way so the future can be better."

Several attempts have been made to establish women's professional basketball leagues in the United States, but, for various reasons, none have taken root. Each has had limited success and short tenure. The WBL was perhaps the most successful, operating for three seasons, but financial difficulties, as with other such attempts, were the primary cause for ruin. These financial troubles have been born out of other maladies. In the past, owners and organizers have never had a well-conceived plan of action. Some former leagues have tried gimmicks like lowering the rims, using different colored basketballs, or having the players jaunt around in skin-tight uniforms—all in the name of marketing and fan attraction. No one has been able to identify and market the women's game for what it is: a well-coached, fundamentally sound, team-oriented game with no Julius Ervings or Michael Jordans to slam dunk the league into the hearts and television screens of its audience. Just about every deception has been created in an attempt to sell women's professional basketball, but no one has ever been able to identify successfully and target the right market under the right circumstances. And no one has thought to consult with Jody Conradt and Pat Summitt or Carol Blazejowski and Ann Meyers.

Ann Meyers, another icon in the history of women's college basketball, is probably most remembered for being the first woman to sign a free agent contract with an NBA team when she signed a pact with the Indiana Pacers in 1980. Was it a gimmick for the downtrodden Pacers? Maybe. But Meyers was more than deserving of the invitation. An All-American at UCLA, Meyers was elected into the Basketball Hall of Fame in 1993. When Meyers was a freshman at UCLA, her big brother, David, was a senior starter on John Wooden's last Bruins national championship squad in 1975. She also participated in track and volleyball during her career at UCLA.

Meyers also had a brief stint with the WBL, when she was the league's number one pick in 1978. Unfortunately, she still had to graduate from UCLA. She played on the silver medal–winning 1976 women's Olympic team, carried the flag for the 1979 Pan American Games, and didn't feel very secure with the WBL at the time. She was considering playing in the 1980 Olympics, and that's when the Pacers called.

"I said to myself, where else am I going to make $50,000," Meyers recalled. "The WBL used it to their advantage because they weren't getting any exposure. But it was at my expense, and I didn't feel very good about the way they did that. I made the Pacers decision before Carter boycotted the Olympics. I figured I had been to the Olympics, and I thought, what if in ten years I say to myself, what if I would have tried out for the Pacers?

"I accepted their offer to try out as a free agent and I signed a one-year personal services contract," Meyers continued. "The situation overseas was just getting started and a lot of girls were apprehensive [about playing overseas]. The Pacers tryout was an opportunity of a lifetime, an opportunity some men don't even get. It was a first and the media was all over that as they are when anything is a first. I think it opened a lot of doors for other people."

Meyers went to the three-day workout but didn't make the team. Fortunately, Meyers' contract was a personal services contract, so even though she didn't make the team, she was still Pacers property. Management moved her upstairs to the broadcasting booth, a move Meyers has never regretted. That's how she got her start in the broadcasting business, which led her to a seventeen-year career as a color commentator and analyst for men's and women's basketball, volleyball, baseball, softball, and tennis. The Pacers released her from her contract, and, although she only earned about $8,200 of the $50,000 in her contract, Meyers's basketball career wasn't yet through.

The year she was released by the Pacers, her WBL rights were traded from Houston to the New Jersey Gems. She signed a three-year contract for $145,000, most of which, according to Meyers, she never received. Her first year (1980–1981) she was the league MVP, but she sat out her second year, which was Blazejowski's first year with the team.

Meyers's move prevented the two future Hall of Famers from ever playing together professionally. Meyers sat out that second season because the Gems had not paid her all the money from the first year of her contract so, in her own words, she took a stand. Her third year was the league's fourth and since it folded, Meyers never received approximately $85,000 of her contracted salary.

"There's a lot of money to be lost in owning a team and operating a league," Meyers said. "I didn't feel the owners treated the players with any respect. They treated us like girls. It was disheartening. I also felt bad because not enough players had sense business-wise. I thought, although I was making a lot of money, other players would see that as the opportunity to make more for themselves. But a lot of players resented my salary. They didn't look at it the way I did. But I don't regret my experience at all."

Meyers doesn't regret her experiences, but she may regret losing the opportunity to make a lot of money overseas. A player of Meyers's credentials and abilities could, in 1995, command a salary in excess of from $200,000 to $300,000 a year in Italy's best women's professional league or in high-paying Japan. The salary comes with a nice condominium or villa to live in and probably a nice car to drive—all at no cost. But as Meyers had alluded, playing overseas was a virgin business in the late 1970s, and no one knew at that time that playing abroad would become as lucrative for women's collegiate players as it has become.

Bruce Levy Associates, in New York City, is the only sports agency that makes most of its income by representing American women's collegiate basketball players and placing them overseas. Bruce Levy Associates places between 50 and 60 of the approximately 100 American women players competing overseas each season. Japan and Italy historically have been the most lucrative markets for American players, but Japan closed its league to foreigners in 1994 until after the 1996 Olympic games are finished. Other countries with women's professional leagues include France, Spain, Israel, Brazil, Germany, Turkey, Portugal, Sweden, and Switzerland—literally worldwide.

Approximately thirty players make more than $50,000 a year, and the elite players (a smaller grouping) can make up to $200,000 or more. The majority of players, though, make less than $50,000. Players in Spain and the Scandinavian countries, for example, make no more than about $20,000. Still, free perks, such as a car and apartment or condominium, can make the cultural experience worthwhile. Most leagues permit two foreign players, which don't necessarily have to be two Americans, although players from the United States are considered the best in the world.

Daedra Charles and Bridgette Gordon have created lucrative and successful careers overseas. The two former Tennessee Lady Volunteers have played primarily in Italy's top league, but Charles experimented with Japan for a year before returning to the top competition in Italy. Both players wish they were able to earn the same lifestyle in the United States that they could afford abroad.

"I wish there was an option to be able to stay home in the States or to go overseas," Charles said. "I'm very family oriented so I would have loved to have stayed home to be around my family and friends and they could see me play. I think there is a lack of support in the States. A lot of people don't want to risk putting money into it [a women's professional league]. Overseas is not for everybody."

Gordon, a member of the 1988 U.S. Olympic team, feels more strongly about this situation than Charles, and she echoes the sentiments of many top women's collegiate players. "It irritates me a lot that there's no professional league in the States," Gordon said. "We invented the game of basketball, but we [women] have to come overseas to play professionally. It's not all about money. The experience of traveling and seeing how people in other cultures live is a great experience. But there's no place like home. I would gladly take a pay cut to play in the states. My family could see me play. And we want to show people how much women's basketball has grown."

Jill Jeffrey, an agent for Bruce Levy Associates, is a former teammate of Blazejowski's with both Montclair State and the Gems. She has been involved in both sides of the basketball business. After her playing career with Montclair and the Gems, Jeffrey turned to coaching and was an assistant at both Northeastern University and Notre Dame before she returned to take the head coaching position at her alma mater. After coaching at Montclair State for seven seasons, she joined Bruce Levy and has been with the firm for approximately five years. Bruce Levy represents both Charles and Gordon.

According to Jeffrey, the situation overseas has not gotten any better for foreign players during the past few years. In 1993 the market changed drastically and faced what Jeffrey termed "total market devastation." Japan closed its doors to foreign women, which displaced about thirty-two top American players into the pool of players trying to get jobs in Europe, and some players were forced into retirement. Also, the recent influx of Eastern European players has made a significant impact. Since the fall of communism, the Eastern European players are free to and willing to accept less compensation, much less than American players would consider—anything to get out of their own countries. Finally, Jeffrey pointed to the economic climate in Europe as a negative factor as well. During a recession, small businesses are hurt tremendously, and these are the companies that sponsor the women's teams. When the business is in trouble, the first discretionary funds to be cut are those to fund the women's basketball club. In Europe, the women's basketball teams are sponsored by many small businesses, unlike Japan where the teams are composed primarily of company employees.

"The different countries have different motives for hiring American players," Jeffrey explained. "In Japan, for example, it's never really difficult for them to field a team from hundreds of thousands of employees, but the problem is the skill level of the Japanese players is so low. That's why they went after the top American players. The interesting point is in the whole history of Americans playing in Japan, only three players have been under 6'1" tall.

"It's obvious they are looking for the tall post players. In their [Japan] decision-making process, 50 percent is the player's technical skills and 50 percent is the player's character. The primary thing the Japanese care about is the company's image. So there's a real select group of American players who have played there.

"The reasons they gave us [for eliminating Americans] were twofold," Jeffrey went on. "They are looking to improve their performance internationally, and they feel having Americans on their teams prevents their players from improving. I've seen a lot of games over there, and they only allow two foreigners on each team, and only one is allowed to play at a time. Both Americans [from opposite teams] are usually guarding each other so I don't really buy that reason. The other reason is more believable. Japan has been experiencing a recession also. These players' salaries keep going up and up each year, and it is difficult for them to justify high salaries for the American players for six months. We expect the league to open back up, but we don't know when. It took the Japanese federation a long time to come to this decision and it won't reverse it quickly."

Six-figure salaries, free cars, and free living accommodations sound nice, but this nomadic lifestyle is not all it's portrayed to be. There are a lot of obstacles and challenges to overcome, and being the American on the team can bring with it more pressure than an NCAA championship game.

"You always have pressure, being the American on the team," Gordon explained. "If you score 50 points, but the team loses by two, you should have scored 53 points so the team could have won by a point. You always could have gotten one more rebound or one more steal. They look to the Americans to do it all. They pay us well to perform, and expect a whole lot. There is pressure every night. I have it a little easier in a sense because I have five players on my team from the Italian national team. We are always under pressure to win because we're the best team in Italy and one of the best in Europe. Everyone wants to beat us. But they still expect me to carry the load, even with three starters from the national team."

The pressure to perform is not the only challenge for the American players. Foreign languages, as well as foreign food, can make for interesting dilemmas. "My first year [in Japan] I wouldn't eat anything that didn't look good or smell right," Charles said. "Japan was a little like America in that they had fast food places all over. But when we ate as a team, that was a different story. The first time they brought out raw fish, I told them politely they had to get some chicken for me and the other American. After a while I tried some things. I learned to sit at the table, bow, eat with chopsticks. I went to school for four months to learn enough [Japanese] to get by. But I didn't know enough to go up to someone on the street and start up a conversation. It was difficult because the Japanese say everything in a correct way, there is no slang.

"In Italy, all of my teammates speak English," Charles continued. "Although I don't know the language that well, I know enough that when I want something, I can ask how much something costs or where the store is. In Japan, nothing sounded like anything. We would play charades and use dictionaries. The other thing was my Japanese teammates wanted to learn English, so they didn't teach us Japanese. If you don't understand what they are saying, it can create a real misconception."

"The language barrier is a big problem," Gordon concurred. "Italian is not a language choice in college. You have Spanish, German, French, Latin. I took Spanish in college, and the two languages are similar so I have had less problems than others. Another difficulty is the stores. They are open nine in the morning until noon, and from 3:30 to eight in the evening. Nothing is open after 8 o'clock. No 24-hour convenience stores, no 7–11s, no gas stations. And the cost of living is much higher here than in the States. Italy has one of the highest costs of living in Europe. The exchange rate goes up and down every day. At home, a dollar is a dollar. And the people here are complicated, very backward. They *think* they know everything."

Still, the life of an American player is not all bad. Gordon, for example, is one of the highest paid players in Italy, and deservedly so. Her living arrangements, as are Charles's, are taken care of, including an apartment and an automobile. Both players admit they basically pay their phone bill, put gas in their cars, and buy food. And with the extensive travel schedule, none of those three bills add up to much in relative terms. They play twice a week: Wednesdays in the European Cup League and Sundays in the Italian League. They practice on Monday, twice on Tuesdays, twice on Thursdays, and once on Friday. Practices, according to both players, are not very intense. Usually about forty-five minutes of the two-hour sessions is actual work, and the rest is talk. The American players usually get a week off to go home for Christmas holidays, but that might be the only vacation for the players in a nine-month stint.

"Women, in general, are treated much differently internationally than they are at home," Jeffrey pointed out. "One experience I had in Japan where we had two clients, one on each team at a scrimmage. It was an informal scrimmage, but the coach of one of the teams actually started pushing and screaming at one of the Japanese players, eventually slapping her in the face. To the Japanese women, that is perfectly acceptable behavior. Whereas the American players were looking at each other, like, 'Oh my goodness.' It is very important that these women know these cultural differences and certainly be aware of what they may face. That preparation and educational aspect prior to them going overseas is really important to their success."

Jeffrey's organization facilitates that process whenever possible. "We put forth a 100 percent effort to do that," Jeffrey said. "It really is an integral part of the player's success, especially initially. There are some players who do better in certain environments and some who will do better in others. We try to create a good marriage between a club and a player so both sides will be happy, and both sides will reach their potential. But that doesn't always happen. Once we recruit and sign a client, I'm going to get to know that player personally as well as technically.

"First we make sure a player will fit technically," Jeffrey continued. "We are not going to convince a team to take a point guard when they need a center. So first we create a technical fit and then we make sure, as far as the culture is concerned, the player will thrive there and not be unhappy. When you take a player, put her overseas a million miles from home, everybody is talking funny, the game is different, the referees aren't on her side, the fan club members aren't around, the coach might not have as much knowledge or experience as her college coach, and maybe she's on a losing team, because those are the teams that hire the top Americans. So all of this is hitting at once. It is very difficult to predict what will happen to the player the first couple of weeks."

Once Jeffrey and her organization match a player to a team, they handle contract negotiations. Bruce Levy Associates requires specific minimum terms for any contract for any player anywhere in the world. Jeffrey calls their contract player-protection oriented. A club must provide these minimum terms for Bruce Levy to even consider placing a player with that club. First and foremost, players are paid in U.S. dollars and the clubs pay the foreign taxes on that money, so the player's salary is net of taxes. Players must be paid one month in advance so, at the end of the season, there are no problems with the player's receiving all of her salary. Players are provided a comfortable, modern apartment and the maintenance is paid by the club. Local transportation is provided, and that varies from country to country. Most players are given the use of an automobile. Round-trip airline tickets, normally two sets, are paid for: one set to get home and back for the season and the other to get home and back for Christmas vacation. Christmas vacation is a paid week of vacation.

There is a bonus system based on team goals rather than on individual performance, comprehensive medical insurance is provided, and free agency is granted at the end of the contract. The contract is a no-cut contract, meaning that, once a player arrives and passes a seven-day trial, the club cannot cut her without paying her for any reason, unless she arrives injured, commits a felony while she is there, or is suspended for several weeks or for more than three games. One last clause would apply if the player were pregnant and unable to play, in which case the team would be allowed to cut her.

These minimum terms are for all Bruce Levy clients, and for the top players, other items might be negotiated. For example, some players have children, so the club might be required to provide childcare and baby-sitting services, or a nanny. All players have access to a phone, but for some of the top players, free phone calls might be an extra included in the contract. Other nuances and idiosyncrasies which aren't included in the contracts often can't be identified until a player arrives and lives through the experience. One experience that players would gladly do without is the outrageous fan behavior.

"Two years ago in the finals they were throwing money and paper airplanes," Gordon said. "Just the other night an official got hit in the head with a coin and suffered a concussion and had to be taken to the hospital. Little kids flip you the finger. They try to spit on you. It's terrible.

"The home fans are great," Gordon went on. "They are very much behind us. I have my own fan club, the Boys of Bridgette. They are the kind of fans I take to heart. I really appreciate our fans, they travel with us. When I was warming up before a playoff game last year, I was watching the stands because the fans were really going at it. The police had their shields on, their blackjacks [nightsticks], mace.

"It was already warm in the gym, before the game, because the fans were going at it. I've had things thrown at me, people try to spit on you when you go to the locker rooms. They say stupid things like, 'Go home.' Last year in a game I was going for a loose ball and this little person is running down the bleachers trying to spit on me."

Women's basketball players would be able to avoid much of this distress if a professional league existed in the United States. Unfortunately, a handful of previous efforts, the most recent being the WBL, have never reached potential.

"I think we will see one again," Texas's Conradt said about attempts for another women's professional league. "The question is will we see a successful one—a financially successful one? I think it's part of that window we are talking about. The opportunity for women's basketball to grow is there. How far it grows and fares at the collegiate level is going to have a direct result on what can happen professionally."

Conradt's counterpart at Tennessee has similar sentiments. "I think in the next ten years we will see another women's pro league in the United States," Tennessee's Summitt said. "I hope I'm still alive. I think money has been the issue and I think along with that I don't think women's basketball had the respect from the media or from fan support [in the past]. We just didn't have the fundamentals in place. Your sport definitely needs to have strong base support in terms of media, fans, and then financial support. It wasn't in place in the past. If you look at collegiate programs now, we are moving in a real positive direction and we are gaining credibility with the media and with spectators and more financial support."

Blazejowski and other former players in the WBL have other thoughts about why those leagues didn't pan out. While Summitt and Conradt have a broader view from a coaching and administrative perspective, former players have a different angle. "I think the leagues that folded, the people were in it for the wrong reasons," Jeffrey lamented. "They thought they were going to turn a profit the first night out."

"We were getting decent salaries, flying on real airplanes, staying in legitimate hotels and playing in legitimate places," recalled Blazejowski. "It was wonderful playing professionally and getting paid. We loved it! But maybe it was a bit before its time. We hadn't gone through enough foundation levels.

"I think the folks that were owners were looking to turn a profit immediately," Blazejowski went on. "They were in it not for the passion of being a basketball enthusiast and trying to help women's basketball. They were in it as opportunists and trying to see it as entertainment and grab the money and run."

No one will be trying to take the money and run in the fall of 1996 when the next two attempts will be made to initiate a professional women's basketball league. Two leagues—the Women's Major Basketball League (WMBL) and the American Basketball League (ABL)—are attempting to tip off their inaugural seasons in the fall of 1996.

The fact that two different leagues are attempting to form is admirable and perhaps indicates the popularity level to which women's basketball has risen. That same fact, however, already spells doom for one or both of the leagues. Are there enough players to form two leagues? Probably. Are there enough coaches to form two leagues? Probably. But the old cliché, you must run before you walk, is applicable here. The United States *is* ready for a women's professional basketball league. It is not ready for two of them. Considering all the variables that go into forming a league, it might have been wiser for the factions from both the WMBL and the ABL to get together, combine their efforts, and develop one league to its fullest potential. Instead, these two leagues will compete against one another for players, coaches, fans, sponsorship dollars, and television time. If all these things are split between the two leagues, the result will be a sport divided. The strength of the effort will be severely weakened. The differences in the two leagues, though, might give one an advantage over the other from the outset. Or it should be said that the differences in the philosophy of the two leagues might give one an advantage.

The WMBL proposes to have franchises with multimillion-dollar budgets, although the money men have not been identified. It is proposing six-figure salaries to players, probably not all players, because players should be compensated according to their talent, skill, and background. The WMBL expects to have teams in eight major cities, but it has not secured any sites, only indicating that it has explored Los Angeles, New York, Chicago, and Houston. Televised games would be a part of the package as well, and the league will be controlled by league ownership—one group would own the entire league. The WMBL planned to have coaches in place in each market by March 1996 with a league-wide draft to be held three months later in June.[5]

The two drawbacks of the WMBL premise is the salary structure for players and the approach to location. Ann Meyers alluded to the negative impact her salary posed to her teammates as well as other players in the Women's Basketball League. And the organizers of the WMBL believe that major markets are the best places to locate these teams. Once again, businesspeople are trying to develop a blueprint without talking to the original architect—like trying to modify the Empire State Building without conferring with the person who poured the foundation.

"You can't compete against a professional team or a major Division I program," Meyers said. "Go to a small town where you're not competing against men's professional teams or major women's college teams. You don't play your games at the Summit (Houston), Madison Square Garden, or the Forum (Los Angeles). Play smaller arenas where things like concessions, security, all those little things will not cost as much. The team that did the best in the WBL was the Chicago Hustle. They played at the arena at DePaul University that holds about 5,000. Even when they didn't sell out, they had 2,000 to 3,000 people there. Tulane is another good place.

"You've got to get your following, you've got to get your communities involved," Meyers continued. "The league has got to be regional; you can't be traveling across the country because it costs too much. Regional play is the most advantageous because you can establish those rivalries. Television has to be involved, and the owners have to be serious about making it a 10–20 year commitment. Finally, women have to be involved in management. Nothing against men, but a statement has to be made to put women in the forefront."

Nine USA Basketball members and twenty-five former top collegians had already signed with the ABL by the fall of 1995, which put a damper on the efforts of the WMBL as far as recruiting top players. The proposed salary range for these players will be from $40,000 (the minimum) to $125,000. The average salary is proposed to be near $70,000, with the upper level reserved for the marquee players. In the fall of 1995, ABL organizers had identified eighteen cities as possible homes for the twelve teams expected to compete. The league claimed to have $4 million in working capital and was working on sponsorship deals, including Nike, as well as a television package. A proposed forty-two-game regular season schedule would be concluded with playoffs in March. League organizers also said the players will own 10 percent of the league.[6]

Lisa Leslie and Sheryl Swoopes, two of the previous three collegiate players of the year had already signed with the league, and 1995 Final Four standout Rebecca Lobo of Connecticut was engaged in contract negotiations as well. Some veteran players of note who had signed included Theresa Weatherspoon, Carla McGhee, Teresa Edwards, and Ruthie Bolton.[7]

The eighteen cities the ABL had investigated had a more grass roots feel to them and certainly had a bit more insight into the mechanics of where a successful league would locate its teams. Six locations were explored for the East Division: Atlanta; Birmingham, Alabama; Hartford or New Haven, Connecticut; Knoxville or Nashville, Tennessee; Orlando, Florida; and Richmond, Virginia. For the Central Division, six destinations were also probed: Cedar Rapids, Iowa; Columbus, Ohio; Indianapolis; Kansas City, Missouri; Minneapolis; and St. Louis. For the West Division, seven locations were examined: Austin, Texas; Denver, Colorado; Portland, Oregon; Seattle; and San Jose, Long Beach, or another Southern California location.[8]

"I think we [the WBL] played in cities where there were too many things happening," said Carol Blazejowski. "The entertainment dollar was really being cut up too much and there just wasn't enough money left to go see a women's professional basketball game. The talent was very good and the games were exciting."

Ever the marketing whiz, Blazejowski has some ideas on how she might promote a women's professional basketball league. "I would start in areas where there is no other show," Blazejowski said. "Market it more as family entertainment. You can bring your kids and your wife, meet the players. Perhaps you could hook up with another pro league that is looking for something to happen in the off season. The Phoenix Suns, for example, have their arena open all year long and they look for things, like indoor lacrosse, to fill half or a quarter of the arena just to cover the bills. And yet the community can embrace it.

"Another way might be to play in areas that already have minor league men's teams, like the CBA (Continental Basketball Association)," Blazejowski continued. "And the people who are involved must look to make a significant investment and to be involved long term, not turn a profit immediately."

Meyers has other, perhaps more creative, marketing ideas, or some might say a little bit unique. "You can't make it like the NBA," Meyers emphasized. "Maybe you play ten-minute quarters instead of twelve minutes. Maybe teams receive points for winning quarters. Maybe you have incentive clauses for leading the team in scoring, rebounding, assists. Do you have the three-point rule? Do you have the foul-out rule, or do you have unlimited fouls and penalize a team after it has exceeded a certain limit? Do you play an overtime period, or play first team to five or seven points wins? There are so many things to think about. You've got to establish your rules first, and you've got to ask yourself, how many players are there going to be on a roster? What about referees?"

One smart thing both the WMBL and the ABL thought through was beginning their inaugural season at the conclusion of the 1996 Summer Olympics in Atlanta. USA Basketball, the United States' governing body for international basketball competition, had placed a great deal of emphasis on the women's basketball team and had made a financial commitment never before made for the American women's team. The excitement following another inspiring college season, quickly followed by the women's competition in the Summer Games, was the perfect catalyst for the two professional leagues to establish their roots.

In years past, both the men's and women's Olympic basketball teams were formed from the top collegians of the previous year. These players would often come together a few months before the Summer Games, practice, and try to meld as a unit in time to win the gold medal. For many years, the athletic superiority and the exceptional skill level possessed by the Americans allowed them to enjoy a good deal of success.

In the 1992 games in Barcelona, Spain, USA Basketball changed all of that when it organized the "Dream Team," a collection of NBA superstars. The United States, long the heavy favorite in most international basketball competitions, had fallen on tough times. Foreign countries began to develop more skilled basketball players, and most foreign countries assembled the best players from their country's professional leagues.

These players were often from six to ten years older than the American collegians, and these adults were stronger, taller, and wiser than their younger American counterparts. Additionally, these foreign players often played as a team for months, many times years, between international competitions, and exhibited a distinct advantage in team chemistry. Finally, the American contingent got tired of playing against the other countries' professionals when, in fact, the United States was still sending true amateurs to the Olympics, in the true spirit of the games.

The Dream Team comprised the best players in America's professional league, the National Basketball Association. This all-star contingent of such players as Michael Jordan, Charles Barkley, Magic Johnson, Patrick Ewing, and Karl Malone was the best collection of basketball players anywhere in the world. Winning the gold medal was a formality.

USA Basketball is trying to follow the lead of the Dream Team for the 1996 games in Atlanta. The 1992 U.S. women's basketball team was thought to be the most talented team at the games, and perhaps the best U.S. team ever. That team settled for the bronze medal. USA Basketball implemented a new formula for the American women's team in an effort to give the American women a bona fide opportunity to win the gold medal. USA Basketball, in 1995, formed the women's national team one year in advance. Twenty-four players reported to the U.S. Olympic Training Center in May to compete for ten spots on the national team.

Two collegians would be added after the 1995–1996 NCAA season was completed. Tara VanDerveer, two-time national champion coach from Stanford University, took a one-year leave of absence from her Cardinal post to coach the team. The women's national team played an exhibition tour against top women's collegiate teams and made an international tour.[9]

This was a gamble by both the players and the organization. The risk for the organization was the hope that it could encourage the best American players to sacrifice from $100,000 to $200,000 they would earn playing overseas for a year in a foreign professional league. In order to lessen the financial blow, USA Basketball paid each of the ten team members a $50,000 salary for the year of training.[10] The other gamble for USA Basketball was whether the experiment would work.

Women's basketball became a recognized Olympic sport in the 1976 games, and the United States had been the women's favorite for a number of years. Entering the 1996 games in Atlanta, however, the USA women had not won the coveted gold since 1988. The first gamble for USA Basketball was successful. The USA's top women's players sacrificed a year of international competition to represent their country and attempt to win the gold medal. Veterans such as Teresa Edwards and Katrina McClain showed that the American women would much rather play for and play in their own country for less money than face the challenges abroad.

By earning a spot on the women's national team, Edwards became the first American player, male or female, to play in four Olympic games. The five foot, eleven inch former University of Georgia All-American has played in Italy, Japan, and Spain and is considered to be one of the best players in the world. She gave up an estimated $100,000 in France to compete for the United States.[11] McClain made the U.S. Olympic team for the third time. The six foot, two inch former University of Georgia All-American is considered to be the best post player in the world. The cost for McClain was an estimated $300,000 in Hungary.[12]

"Basketball is basketball, regardless of gender, race, or age," Meyers concluded. The women's edge is they do the fundamentals. It's a great game. The men's game has gotten out of hand a little bit. They carry the ball, they travel. They've gotten away from fundamentals. The taunting, the fights, the trash talking. I don't think there's anyplace for it in the game.

"The women's game is still in a position to be willing to do things for their game. They are still trying to promote themselves. Do you think you would see a major men's program set time aside after a game for players to give autographs to little kids?"

Meyers's insight, ironically, is not reserved for women's basketball. Her philosophy carries over to the few women's professional sports leagues in the United States. Despite her unassuming assessment of the difference between the genders' pursuit of the round ball, Meyers's thoughts point to some of the drawbacks evident in women's professional sports.

7

The Professional Dilemma

Why has it taken so long for Title IX to be enforced? It's the old boy network at work. It's the same thing when tennis was opened up and the men wanted to close us out. Men are not going to cooperate unless they are forced to.

—Billie Jean King

Mahwah, New Jersey, is hardly the best-known stop on the women's professional tennis tour. But against the picturesque backdrop of the Ramapo Mountains in the northwest corner of the Garden State, tennis promoter extraordinaire John Korff has built himself a miniature tennis empire. Going on twenty years, Korff has developed, packaged, and popularized an event called the Pathmark Tennis Classic. Learning a number of lessons from the Women's Tennis Association (WTA) on how not to do business, Korff has utilized that information and combined his marketing savvy to produce an event that rivals most WTA events in popularity (for players and fans) and revenue production.

"I used to direct a number of women's tennis tournaments," Korff said from his office in the Sheraton Crossroads complex. "But Pathmark has been the only one now for more than ten years. It makes more business sense to focus on one event. If you're not entrenched in the community where the event is held, it's tough to make a tournament a happening. The other tournaments were a lot of fun, but they didn't make good business sense."

Tour players often alter their schedules in order to participate in the Mahwah event. Over the years, Korff has attracted many of the top players, including Steffi Graf, Gabriela Sabatini, Mary Pierce, Monica Seles, Mary Joe Fernandez, Jennifer Capriati, and Lisa Raymond. Since 1992 Korff has begun the tournament with an exhibition of top men's players for the benefit of the Safe Passage Foundation, a charitable organization founded by the late tennis great Arthur Ashe. Pete Sampras, Andre Agassi, and John McEnroe have all played in that exhibition. As the tournament approaches its twentieth year in Mahwah, more and more top players make time to participate.

"It has become increasingly easier to attract the top players because the money is there," Korff explained. "More importantly, the players really like it here. You really can't pay a player to do something she doesn't want to do. And we have credibility from former players. Our biggest competition [for getting players] is the player who wants to take some time off. We don't have a problem getting players.

"The players like the tournament for a number of reasons," Korff continued. "The longevity, it's been around for a long time, and when players see that they think it's important. Second, I know most of them, and we're pretty laid back and we don't hassle them. We treat them as eighteen- to twenty-five-year-olds. I'm friends with the players and their friends trust me. It's an unusual trust relationship. We don't treat them like they walk on water. There is less tension here. You can create artificial tension. If you create tension among your staff, the staff feels it and the players feel it. Our focus is on everybody having fun and so we defuse a lot of the angst players have."

This is much more than tennis, though. For $8.00 you can have your car parked by a valet, and the secured lots are loaded with BMWs, Jaguars, Mercedes Benzes, and Lincolns. The common folks park out behind the corporate hospitality tents. Korff has attracted between 200 and 300 corporate sponsors who support his nearly $2 million expense account (including the purse).[1] Many of the sponsors have direct contact with potential customers. You can sit in a brand new Saab automobile, sample the latest cereal from General Mills, taste the newest in chilled, bottled coffee, and the list goes on. Spectators can literally fill up a couple of shopping bags (and they often do) as well as their stomachs as the sponsors take advantage of this rare opportunity for personal contact.

"This tournament relies less on the athletes and more on the business and ancillary activities," Korff said. "The on-court action is the hook to allow everything else to happen, and they play off each other. If all you focus on is the players, then business suffers. If all you focus on is the business, then the players suffer.

"At first, sponsors would say, who are you?" Korff went on. "Now they have heard of it, they are aware of it, they consider it to be a big deal. The challenge now is that people think we are for real, they want us to prove to them that we are for real by coming across with the things they require."

Huge twenty-foot blow-up balloons of Tony the Tiger, the Oreo Cookie, Miller Genuine Draft (beer bottle), and Pepsi-Clear (bottle) can be seen from the nearby highway chaos, and later in the day fans can take a hot-air balloon ride in another facsimile of the Frosted Flakes mascot. This is more than tennis. This is big business, but it is customer friendly. The spectators who flock to this splendid hotel complex are treated first class in every respect.

Fans have opportunities rarely seen on the WTA tour. They get to have close contact with the players, and the players, more comfortable under the attentiveness of Korff and his staff, are relaxed and willing to oblige. It is commonplace here for players to stop on the way back to the hotel after a match or practice to sign autographs.

After an early-round match in July 1993, for example, top seed Mary Joe Fernandez and her opponent Heidi Sprung tossed armfuls of Pathmark Tennis Classic frisbees into the stands. They both also hit a number of tennis balls from the match into the stands. Finally, Fernandez played a twelve-point exhibition match with a young fan, Debbie, from Wayne, New Jersey. Fernandez good-naturedly offered her young opponent some pointers and obviously enjoyed the opportunity to give her young challenger a moment on center court.

Korff took the event off the WTA tour in 1989 and made it into an exhibition. This made player recruitment a bit more difficult because Korff must hold the tournament on an "off week" for the WTA tour if he wants the top players to participate. One year, the WTA fined Top 100 players who played in Korff's event. Another change Korff made was to relocate the event from the venue it had occupied for its first fifteen years, Ramapo College.

"First we had to solve the problems of being at Ramapo," Korff explained. "As the event grew, we outgrew the college. I wanted to stay in Bergen County, and I didn't want to leave Mahwah. That was a major element. Then we had to get over the obstacle of people thinking we were just a local tennis tournament, and make people realize we are a New York tristate event. And we've done that. Third, we had to have the ability to attract players; we had to be freed of the WTA shackles to let players play in the tournament.

"We needed more permanence," Korff said of the move. "We don't have traffic jams anymore and we have between two and three thousand underground parking spaces. We have a lot more logistical plusses in our current location. And we are at a venue where the people are for-profit, they want to make money. The college is a different mentality. Here [at the Crossroads] they say, 'How can we use the tennis tournament to make money?' At the college, they said, 'Is it five o'clock yet?'

In addition to attracting top players and numerous corporate sponsors, Korff has attracted ABC Television to broadcast the event for nearly five years now. He also has had a commitment from the SportsChannel, which helps the tournament reach a much larger audience, including sixty-three foreign countries.

He begins promoting the event more than thirteen months in advance, and part of this strategy is to lure potential sponsors. Korff believes that the best way to entice sponsors is to let them see the event up close and personal. It takes four months to plan the physical part, November through January for the promotion plan, with implementation beginning the February before the event. Ticket sales and creating hype follow shortly after the promotion plan is set in motion.

Korff has had more than forty-eight products on-site and has bought more than 1,200 radio spots in the expensive New York market. Korff often throws advertising time into the sponsorship packages. He owns all the television time reserved for the tournament so sponsors do not have the added expense of purchasing advertising.

"Sponsors can give you one of three things," the Harvard MBA graduate said. "One of the things is money. The second is the opportunity for other things, like distribution of information through their products or in their stores. The third thing is credibility. Our increased level of sponsorship has enabled us to do a lot of upgrading.

"I don't consider this an opportunity to get my tennis tournament on television," Korff said. "I went to them [ABC Sports] and asked, 'How can we turn this into a revenue source for you?' We've come up with a formula where we can make a bunch of money and they can make a bunch of money. It has helped give us a lot of credibility. When people show up here and see all these television cameras, they are impressed. We just think of things differently. We just figure out how we can make money for people."

The shortcomings of the tournament are minimal. In an effort to keep the bottom line tidy, Korff relies exclusively on volunteers for logistics, like setup and takedown, ticket sales, and seating. He also invests very little in public relations, although he could generate more visibility if he made a concerted effort in this area. The other drawback, for pure tennis fans, is Pathmark's field of twenty-eight players. Only a handful are the top players in the world; the rest are a combination of up-and-comers and marginal has-beens. As a result, the competition level is abysmal until the quarter- or semifinal rounds.

That is not really much different from the situation in the WTA tour events, where a minority of players control the victory stand. This is just one of the factors that has led to the downturn in popularity of women's professional tennis over the last half decade. The challenges to women's professional sports here are not so much from the old boys' network, although that has been a factor in the past. The obstacles in women's professional sports today have been created by the sports themselves.

Granted, at the Grand Slam tennis events, the only events where the men and women compete at the same venue, the prize money is greater for the men in three of those tournaments than for the women. In October 1995, the Australian Open announced an increase in the men's purse more than the women's purse for the 1996 tournament. With that announcement, the Australian became the third of the four Grand Slam events to offer a larger purse for the men's players than the women's.[2] The French Open and Wimbledon are the other two. Ironically, the U.S. Open is the only Grand Slam event to offer equal prize money for both genders.

According to *USA Today* research data, as of February 1994, more than 166 male golfers and 137 male tennis players have career earnings of $1 million or more, whereas only 56 female golfers and 46 female tennis players have earned $1 million or more.[3]

"When we're together at major events, I think equal money is correct," King said. "The guys say we only play the best two of three sets and they play the best three of five sets. But actually our bodies are better suited to play five sets. Arthur Ashe was going to do an article a number of years ago on why women are weaker and can't play three out of five. Which was the men's argument. When Arthur found out the facts, that was the end of the article."

In 1968 King won £750 as the women's singles champion at Wimbledon, and men's champion Rod Laver garnered £2,000. "It was a huge effort going over to speak to the All England Lawn and Tennis Club," King recalled. "Sitting there, I told Jerry [Diamond, WTA executive director at the time] to talk because they wouldn't listen to a woman. We got 70 percent of the men's purse, but it was a huge effort just to get some kind of compromise. I don't think women should worry so much about equal prize money at those big tournaments. I say, let's try to get the best we can. We are different products, different markets."

Women's professional tennis is not what it once was—the premier professional sport for the female gender—for four main reasons. First and foremost, fan interest has waned because of the lack of rivalry. There is no marquee matchup that tennis fans anticipate with great fervor. Second, the tour went without a title sponsor for two years, from 1993–1995. Past sponsors Kraft General Foods and Virginia Slims not only were sponsors, they provided public relations, event management, and a host of other duties that the WTA had to take on itself. Third, unlike the mature, gracious competitors of the past, today's women's tennis players are seen by many as inaccessible, spoiled brats. Finally, compounding the first dilemma, there is no great American player. While this is a cyclical phenomenon, the lack of a dominant American creates disinterest in the powerful media, especially television.

This is not exactly what King envisioned in the early 1970s when she labored to organize the WTA. In 1970 Phillip Morris sponsored the first women's tournament, the Virginia Slims of Houston, for a total prize of $7,500. In 1973 King and a handful of others spearheaded the formation of the WTA in order to give women's professional players more power and control of their sport in terms of sponsorship and prize money.

"I thought we needed to have one voice and to play under one umbrella," King said. "We wanted to improve the conditions because this was our livelihood. We signed one-dollar contracts with Gladys [Heldman, publisher of *World Tennis* magazine at the time] and we were all suspended from our contracts with our associations. We had nine players originally. We were ostracized from within. It was definitely a dividing wedge. We had opposition from a lot of different areas. It was a very difficult, tumultuous, fearful time for all of us. Everyone thought it was so exciting, but it wasn't what the public perceived."

King actually began thinking about an association in 1964. At the time, the women's players didn't play for prize money. The top four seeds at a tournament were given per diems. In 1971 the United States Tennis Association responded with a USTA circuit, so the women were divided between the WTA and the USTA. In 1971 the women competed for a total purse of $250,000, for the entire season, and King won the lion's share;

she became the first professional female athlete to earn more than $100,000 in a single year ($117,000).

"In 1968, when tennis became an open sport, men tried to squeeze us out," King said. "It was an old boys' network type of thing. You had male promoters and the male players were saying to the male promoters, why are we giving the women anything, we don't need them."

King became the pilot for the women's push for recognition and acceptance. Women's tennis couldn't have asked for a better ambassador. She was ranked number one in the world five times between 1966 and 1972, and she was ranked first on the U.S. doubles list for a record twelve years. She won thirty-nine Grand Slam titles, including a record twenty Wimbledon titles combined (singles, doubles, and mixed doubles). She is just one of eight players to hold a singles title in each of the grand slam events. In 1987 she was inducted into the International Tennis Hall of Fame.

King's straight-set victory over self-proclaimed male chauvinist Bobby Riggs in 1973 was perhaps one of her most significant victories. The event was held in the Houston Astrodome, and the crowd of 30,472 is still the largest audience to view a tennis match. Las Vegas made Riggs an 8–5 favorite, despite Riggs's twenty-six-year seniority in age (fifty-five years old to King's twenty-nine).

"We were pretty much nonexistent in the mind of the public," King said. "We were given a negative view from the media. But in 1973 I played Riggs, we formed the WTA, we got a CBS contract in 1974, and Chris Evert was coming along as a star and a lot of people could identify with her 'girl next door' persona. Martina defected and she was a tennis player and a great athlete. Phillip Morris and their public relations people really hounded the media. All those factors coming together really helped.

"1973 was very significant, it was a big year for men and women," King went on. "We really got excited. The Riggs match put tennis on the map. Participation went way up. But the tennis industry didn't pay attention, and that's why growth didn't continue. We [tennis] could have been huge."

Perhaps the industry didn't capitalize because it got lazy, and who could find blame with that idle behavior? The tennis world was about to be mesmerized, engaged, and enchanted by one of the most intriguing, lengthy rivalries in sports history.

Chris Evert made her professional debut in 1972 and quickly made her presence felt by winning four tournaments at the young age of eighteen. Martina Navratilova would play in the 1975 U.S. Open and never return to her native Prague in the Czech Republic. Together these two players, with contrasting styles, would stage a fifteen-year rivalry, unprecedented today and equaled only, perhaps, by the Magic Johnson–Larry Bird warfare in the National Basketball Association during the 1980s.

Evert was the cool, confident, graceful master of the baseline with the wholesome appearance and gracious demeanor. She was the American favorite. Navratilova was the epitome of physical conditioning, and she blended her athleticism with her tenacious serve-and-volley style of play. Early in her career, Navratilova could fall victim to her nerves in tight situations, and she was the defector from Eastern Europe. The two had a profound effect on each other as well.

Navratilova's physical conditioning and strength motivated Evert to improve her own physical fitness, and Navratilova's patience, confidence, and demeanor improved significantly over the course of their careers. Ironically, the two became and remain good friends.

Evert and Navratilova are the only women's tennis players to record more than 1,000 career victories. From November 1975 until August 1987, all but twice, Evert or Navratilova was ranked number one in the world in women's singles. They faced each other fourteen times for Grand Slam titles and eighty times overall over a seventeen-year span. Navratilova holds a 43–37 overall edge, and that advantage was secured by winning the last thirteen times consecutively the two played. The pair even teamed together to win two Grand Slam doubles titles: the 1975 French Open and the 1976 Wimbledon.

Evert set the standard with 157 career singles titles and retired in 1989 after the U.S. Open. From 1972 to 1989 she was never ranked lower than fourth in the season-ending ratings. Evert has the highest career winning percentage, .900, and she is third in career winnings with nearly $9 million. Evert owned the French Open; she won the singles title there seven times to highlight her eighteen career Grand Slam titles.

Several years Evert's junior, Navratilova distinguished herself with a record nine Wimbledon singles titles and broke Evert's career mark of 157 titles by winning 166 of her own. She is head and shoulders above her nearest challenger for career money with nearly $20 million. Navratilova further distinguished herself by becoming the preeminent doubles player, winning an unprecedented 163 doubles championships. She broke Evert's ten-year-old record of fifty-five consecutive victories by winning seventy-four straight victories in 1984. She also won eighteen career Grand Slam singles titles. It is difficult to envision that such a competition will ever happen again. For approximately fifteen years, Evert and Navratilova won a remarkable 323 singles titles between them.

A similar competition was brewing in the early 1990s between Steffi Graf and Monica Seles. Graf turned pro in 1982, but she didn't win her first Grand Slam title until 1987 and then began to dominate the circuit, capturing the elusive Grand Slam (Australian Open, French Open, Wimbledon, U.S. Open) in 1988. With Evert retiring the following year and with Navratilova beyond the dominance of her brilliant run, Graf became virtually unbeatable from 1988 to 1990 winning eight Grand Slam titles during that stretch.

Seles joined the tour in 1989, won her first Grand Slam title in 1990, and then the native of Novi Sad, Yugoslavia, exploded. She captured six Grand Slam titles in the next two years, including winning back-to-back titles at the Australian, French, and U.S. Open. She defeated Graf in three of those finals. Tragedy would postpone this growing rivalry in 1993. After winning her third consecutive Australian Open, Seles was competing in a tournament in Hamburg, Germany. During a changeover in her quarter-final match with Magdalena Maleeva, a thirty-eight-year-old, unemployed lathe operator, Guenter Parche, stabbed Seles in the back, just below the left shoulder blade. Parche, a self-professed Graf fanatic, wanted Graf to hold the number one ranking held by Seles at the time.

Although the physical wound healed, the psychological scars kept Seles away from the game for two and a half years. During Seles's absence, from April 1993 until her return to Grand Slam action in the 1995 U.S. Open, Graf won six Grand Slam titles to boost her career total to eighteen to tie her with Evert and Navratilova on the all-time list. Appropriately, in her first tour action since her injury, Seles swept through the field at the 1995 Open, only to find Graf waiting for her in the finals. Graf captured the 7–6, 0–6, 6–4 decision.

The year 1993 was not a good one for the WTA. The Seles tragedy was the focus for many, but other calamities compounded the loss of the sport's top-ranked player and shifted attention to the continuing practice of immature teenagers joining the WTA tour only to be engulfed by media exposure and financial freedom.

Many experts thought Jennifer Capriati would be the next great American player. Having joined the tour just three weeks before her fourteenth birthday in 1990, Capriati had already been to the semifinals of the French Open, U.S. Open, and Wimbledon by the age of fifteen. At age sixteen she defeated Graf for the Olympic gold medal at the 1992 games and had accumulated career earnings of $1.5 million.

In 1993, however, Capriati struggled with personal demons. Many felt she had joined the tour at too young an age. She seemed to lack motivation and didn't perform to expectations. When Seles was struck down, Capriati had an opportunity to step in and fill the void and possibly create another Evert-Navratilova style rivalry by challenging Graf for supremacy. Instead, Tampa police cited Capriati in December 1993 for allegedly shoplifting jewelry in a mall. Five months later, in May 1994, Capriati was arrested for possession of marijuana. Later that year, Capriati took a leave of absence from the tour. Media reports had hinted at potential comebacks on several occasions, but as of December 1995, Capriati had not returned to the tour full time.

In July 1993, Mary Pierce, then eighteen years old, obtained a restraining order against her father, Jim, further highlighting the dilemma of the teenage tennis star being pushed by an overzealous parent. Jim Pierce, known for verbally abusing his daughter, her opponents, and other spectators, was banned from tennis events by the Women's Tennis Council.[4] At the Pathmark Tennis Classic that summer, photos of Jim Pierce were circulated to all security personnel and gatekeepers in an effort to keep him from attending matches at the nontour event.

To further compound the negative news in 1993, Phillip Morris, parent company for Kraft Foods and Virginia Slims, announced that Kraft would no longer be the tour sponsor after 1993 and that Virginia Slims would relinquish its role in 1994. Corporation officials cited financial reasons for the withdrawal. One has to wonder if the WTA took a page from Korff's management style if Kraft wouldn't still be the title sponsor. Korff doesn't just take from his sponsors, he turns his relationship with his corporate partners into a win–win situation. By losing the title sponsor and then taking two years to find a suitable replacement, the WTA lost some of its identity and lost some of its credibility as well as some of its visibility.

In 1971 the total purse for the season, sponsored by Virginia Slims, was $250,000. The purse surpassed $1 million for the first time in 1974, but this was for the entire circuit, not just one tournament. In 1983 Virginia Slims sponsorship rose to more than $10 million and reached $15 million in 1987. In 1989 Virginia Slims completed its tenure as sole tour sponsor but still remained responsible for the Virginia Slims tournaments, which were part of the WTA tour. In 1990 Kraft General Foods took over as title sponsor, and the 1990 tour played for a pot of $23 million. In Kraft's final year of sponsorship in 1993, the total purse was more than $33 million. In 1994 more than $35 million in purses was available for sixty-two events in twenty-two countries.

In 1994 the WTA signed a $16 million contract with IMG, a Cleveland-based sports marketing firm, to represent the tour in marketing and television rights negotiations. In October 1995, the WTA changed its official name to the WTA Tour and signed a three-year deal with Corel Corporation as its worldwide sponsor. The deal is worth $12 million, but one has to wonder what impact a marketer of computer graphics and multimedia software will have from its home base in Canada.[5]

"The perception is that we're [women's tennis] on the way down," King said. "That we're hard to reach, that the players are brats—and they are. They [the public] think we're going down, but we have more grass roots programs now than ever. The United States is down right now, but everything runs in cycles. Europe is up. I believe everything goes on cycles. Right now, I think everybody wants something new."

The WTA made a move in the right direction by asking King and Evert to join their board of directors as advisors. Still, King's organization, World TeamTennis (WTT), does more to promote and enhance women's and men's tennis than either of the other two professional circuits. World TeamTennis is divided into three divisions: the Professional League, the Recreational League, and Junior TeamTennis.

The Professional League has twelve teams playing in three divisions (East, Central, West) across the country. East teams are located in Atlanta, Charlotte, New Jersey, and Sarasota, Florida; Central teams are found in Kansas City, San Antonio, St. Louis, and Wichita; the West teams reside in Boise, Newport Beach, Phoenix, and Sacramento. Each team is coed, with three men and three women, and plays fourteen matches, half at home and half away. There is a maximum of three playoff matches, including the national championship, which has been televised by ESPN. The season lasts five weeks, usually the time period in early July to through early August between Wimbledon and the U.S. Open. Marquee players include Bjorn Borg, Jimmy Connors, Navratilova, and Zina Garrison Jackson.

More important is the manner in which these players are compensated. They are awarded prize money only as a team. The league signs the players, not the teams. And the teams are franchised, like Domino's Pizza. The WTT is the only professional sport that operates in this manner. The league signs the players so there are no bidding wars. When King recruited Jimmy Connors to play, there weren't twelve cities bidding for Connors's services. Each team contributes the same amount of prize money, and each team knows what it is contributing. Prize money is awarded based on the percentage of games won.

The Recreational League is a year-round grass roots coed program for people of all ages and skill levels. It is, according to King, the fastest growing recreational tennis program in the country. Since its start in 1985, more than 340,000 athletes in 1,600 cities have participated. Leagues are played in public parks, tennis facilities, college campuses, and military bases. Recreational players have direct access to the national office in Chicago via toll free lines, and they also receive *Point of Contact*, the official World TeamTennis newsletter, three times per year. The national office holds a minimum of ten recreational days per year, which include appearances by King and other WTT stars, press conferences, clinics, and WTT demonstrations.

Junior TeamTennis is similar in concept to the Recreational League; however, it is designed for boys and girls eighteen years of age and under. The format allows for all skill levels and different age groups. Junior leagues, known as Junior TeamTennis challenges, are played in public parks, tennis facilities, and schools. More than 15,000 juniors have participated across the country, and the challenges begin at the local level and proceed to a state and regional event. Junior participants also receive *Point of Contact* four times a year.

"I want World TeamTennis to work so badly so that children growing up get to see men and women working together," King said. "Not dependent on one or the other, but people growing up interdependent. They've [children] got to see that there's got to be equal contribution to the effort.

"If there's a little girl in the stands watching, she will think it is normal for men and women to be on the same team working toward a common goal . . . all the things boys have been taught all along."

While women's tennis has struggled with its identity and its public, women's professional golf has quietly continued to strengthen its foundation as well as gain an enviable grass roots following. Much of this has to do with the manner in which the Ladies Professional Golf Association (LPGA) conducts its business. While not considered as glamorous as their tennis counterparts, women's professional golfers have built a substantial niche through diligence and vision.

In 1944 three women began what was then labeled the Women's Professional Golf Association (WPGA). After struggling for a number of years, Wilson Sporting Goods signed on as a supporter, and the tour renamed itself the Ladies Professional Golf Association (LPGA) in 1950. With just seven events and only $50,000 in prize money, the first year of the new organization, players couldn't earn much money, let alone make a living.

Nearly ten years later, the tour expanded to twenty-six tournaments, and total prize money rose to $200,000. Hall of Fame players like Babe Zaharias, Louise Suggs, and Betsy Rawls gave the tour some recognizable personalities and gave the tour credibility and a growing following among the public and the media.

Mickey Wright educated the growing public perception as she won forty-five tournaments in a four-year span from 1961 to 1964, and television recognized the escalating popularity of women's golf with its first broadcast of an event in 1963. Sears and Roebuck became the first sponsor of the tour and others followed shortly after. By the end of the decade, the tour had grown to thirty-four events, and prize money increased to $600,000, or an average of $17,650 per event.

The 1970s signaled some unsettling times for the organization when financial difficulties threatened the strides the tour continued to take. A new commissioner in the middle of the decade, Ray Volpe, reorganized the infrastructure of the organization and developed a board of directors, a players council, and separate divisions to deal specifically with corporations, sponsors, and the media.

In the early 1980s, the LPGA was again on solid financial ground. Total prize money grew to $6.4 million, and the tournament fields nearly doubled from 60 to more than 120 players for each event. The other major factor in the continued success and popularity of the LPGA was television. In the early 1980s, the LPGA went from two television events to fourteen.

In 1994 LPGA players competed for total prize money of nearly $22 million in thirty-seven events. Even with this continuing progress, however, one needs only to compare the prize money on any given weekend between the LPGA tournament participants and their counterparts in the men's Professional Golf Association (PGA) or even the men's Senior Tour to recognize that inequalities still exist.

"We have not had as much leverage as the PGA tour," said Ty Votaw, special assistant to former commissioner Charles S. Mechem, Jr. "We don't really look at the disparity in purses although it's difficult not to. We like to look at how we do in relation to the men and make that comparison in how women in other sports compare to men in other sports.

"Their [PGA] purses are higher than ours, but they also play more than we do," Votaw continued. "We are purely sponsor-driven. The sponsor's main responsibility to the LPGA is to pay the purse. They are also responsible for operating expenses and they retain all the revenue."

LPGA sponsors vary from corporate giants to community groups, charitable organizations, and local chambers of commerce. This is one of the factors that has given the LPGA its widespread appeal.

"One aspect where we are different is that some of the cities [in which] we are most successful are off the beaten track," Votaw explained. "Such as Rochester and Corning, New York, and Toledo and Youngstown, Ohio. We are in Chicago and Los Angeles, but those middle markets are very important to us."

Another ingredient responsible for the positive relationship the LPGA has with its supporters is the disposition of the players. "I think it's an accurate perception that we have a more intimate relationship with the communities where we have our tournaments," Votaw said. "That's the feedback that I get from people. I've received letters from people over the last three-and-a-half years who have played in pro-ams on both tours. Not to slam our male counterparts, but people say they have a better time, more fun and our players are more personable. Our players are accessible. That trickles down in a lot of ways. We work with attitude with our players. Because of that acceptability and the enthusiasm we have, when we come to town, the town is glad to see us and welcomes us with open arms."

Votaw believes these characteristics not only pose a dividing line between the LPGA and its male counterparts, but also separate the LPGA from other women's professional sports as well.

"Again, not to slam women's tennis, but I think our atmosphere does separate us from women's tennis," Votaw said. "One of the things they [the WTA] are facing now is the boomerang effect of their star system. They have two or three stars and then the name recognition drops off. Also, their stars are teenagers, so by their own admission they are trying to find their own identity. We may not have a star with the international status of Monica [Seles] or Steffi [Graf], but we have more depth and the quality of stars is much greater. You combine that with the accessibility, and you get, I hate to use a cliché, a warm fuzzy feeling from our events. And we are often a big fish in a small pond. Those events that are on television or covered by the media mean a lot to that particular community."

And, unlike the tennis industry in the early to mid-1970s which, according to Billie Jean King, ignored the opportunity to grow, the LPGA has made every effort to capitalize on its status. In 1959 the LPGA developed the LPGA Teaching and Club Professional Division (T&CP). This branch comprises golf directors, head professionals, teaching professionals, assistant professionals, owners of golf schools and driving ranges, high school and college coaches, and golf administrators. By developing and executing creative teaching and educational and special event programs throughout the country, the T&CP Division has made its presence known throughout the golf industry.

Some of the activities this group has organized in recent years include the LPGA golf clinics for women (sponsored by Gillette), the LPGA teaching schools, the National Golf Foundation/LPGA "Strategies for Effective Teaching and Coaching" workshops, and the Women in Golf Summit national conference, a national seminar. These activities are designed to assist those who teach women's golf to perform their duties to the highest degree possible.

Another integral segment of the LPGA's focus on communities, and another program administered by the T&CP Division, is LPGA Junior Golf. The division started Junior Golf in 1989 with a grant from the Amateur Athletic Foundation. The program is designed for minority and underprivileged children to learn the game of golf, develop an understanding of the game, and appreciate the fundamentals of play. T&CP personnel, as well as other teaching professionals, instruct these young people not only in basics of the game but also golf etiquette, rules, proper dress, and golf course management.

Los Angeles was the site of the original program, and it now has gained the financial backing of corporations such as Sprint, Oldsmobile, and Budget Rent-a-Car. The LPGA Foundation is the fund-raising arm for this program. Two other programs were recently developed, using Los Angeles as the model, in Portland, Oregon, and in Detroit. Plans are under way to expand this unique opportunity to other cities. Both Portland and Detroit received an incredible amount of support from large corporations in their communities.

"Other things we do that don't get as much publicity is the grass roots effort," Votaw said. "We're not doing it for the public relations, and it's another activity that doesn't go to the bottom line. Any money sponsors might donate to it goes directly to The LPGA Foundation to maintain the operating budget for those programs. The Foundation was set up specifically to operate those programs.

"We also have LPGA junior girls golf clubs in more than forty-nine cities in the United States as well as clubs in Canada, Australia, and New Zealand," Votaw went on. "Boys are expected to compete early on, but our studies show girls shun competition at an early age. The junior golf club is designed for girls who would like to take up golf, but competition is not the reason they come out. We take the approach to learn the game of golf as a lifetime sport. We try to develop in them a warmth and affection for the game of golf in a nonthreatening way. These are ways to give back to the community."

The first Junior Golf Club was introduced in Phoenix in 1989 and is designed for girls from six to eighteen years of age. The clubs differ from other junior programs in that each event has a theme, such as the Turkey

Shoot, Derby Day, and the Mother/Daughter Clinic. Fun is the main focus, and the instruction is extensive. LPGA players are also involved in the Pen Pal Program where tournament players and participants in the Junior Golf program write to each other. LPGA players also participate in the "Don't Throw It, Give It," program through which professional players give to the juniors used golf apparel, golf shoes, golf gloves, and golf balls. Finally, in 1992, Gatorade signed on as sponsor of the LPGA Junior Clinic program now sponsored by Crayola. Through the efforts of LPGA players, in co-ordination with the T&CP members, junior golfers are taught the fundamentals of golf through clinics at various tour sites throughout the country all during the season.

"We're not trying to simply say, our players are great people and that's why you should come out and watch them play," Votaw said. "They are great golfers, first of all, and the results of their ability are closer to the average amateur. The average golfer is not going to learn from watching John Daly hit three-hundred yard drives. They will admire it. But the things our players do are more closely related to the amateur golfer. Our players use fairway woods. Most amateurs have to use fairway woods. Course management, fairway woods, these are elements the amateur golfer can relate to. We try to bring things to the people that they can appreciate."

Despite the high quality of play, the grass roots efforts, and the charitable donations (both the WTA and the LPGA support charitable organizations), the final yardstick these professionals would like to be judged by would-be television exposure. Going into the 1994 season, the LPGA had seventeen tournaments, less than half of all their events, on television, only nine of which were on network television. With the advent of the Golf Channel in January 1995, the LPGA had twenty-eight tournaments televised. The WTA has fewer events televised than the LPGA, but it has an advantage when they gain exposure at the major events with their male counterparts.

"We would love to have more events on television," Votaw concluded. "In theory, television is another barometer by which we are measured."

Now, if men could only learn to appreciate the women who report on sports.

8

The Last Male Bastion

Ain't no woman sportscaster who can tell me what it's like to get hit
by a blitzing linebacker from the blind side. She never played the game.
—Joe Six-pack

There may be no other situation in which a woman is challenged more
frequently and more vehemently by men than sportswriting and sports-
casting. There might not be anything more embarrassing for a male than
to learn that a female knows more about sports than he does. Males believe
their entire gender was born with infinite wisdom about sports, any sports—
from football to yachting to auto racing. Men consider sports knowledge
hereditary, congenital. Name the sport and Bobby Beergut will recite a
litany of statistics that will impress the most ardent fan, not to mention send
his chums at Joe's Bar & Grill spinning on their barstools.

It is a virtual guarantee that at most establishments, such as the fictional
Joe's, when a female sportscaster appears on the large-screen television, the
volume is turned down until the guy reappears. The woman couldn't possibly have anything to contribute that the local fan club doesn't already
know. Or, not to make such disapproval obvious, a channel changer will
keep the sound off for the entire pregame show because, once the game
starts, the woman will not be heard from again until half-time, when the
sound goes off again.

Since the first female sports journalist made her debut in the early 1970s, no group has been met with as much resistance. Men have felt all along that women sports journalists simply do not have the knowledge to report on the topic. That attitude was, and to a lesser degree still is, strictly based on gender. Men feel that since no woman has ever been sacked by Greg Lloyd, never smacked a Greg Maddux slider, or never crushed a golf ball 350 yards like John Daly, women simply cannot relate to that experience or provide an accurate description of the act.

Network television did nothing to eliminate that stereotype. In the mid- to late 1970s and early 1980s, CBS Sports started their National Football League broadcast every Sunday with the "NFL on CBS" pregame show. The telecast featured Brent Musberger, ex-NFL player Irv Cross, and prognosticator Jimmy "the Greek" Snyder, along with Jayne Kennedy and Phyllis George. Kennedy and George were rarely, if ever, given substantial stories on which to report. Their significant knowledge of the subject matter was lacking and, consequently, they rarely had anything important to contribute. George, a former beauty pageant winner, and Kennedy were both physically attractive, but they did not have the ability to provide meaningful information, and the entire population of female sports journalists lost credibility and was incorrectly categorized. Some women in the industry now negatively refer to this phenomenon as the Phyllis George–Jane Kennedy Syndrome.

Equally difficult for female sports journalists was the lack of cooperation and support they got from male colleagues, as well as the teams, athletes, and coaches on which they reported. Male sports journalists, favorably depicted by the Oscar Madison character played by Jack Klugman in the "Odd Couple" sitcom, perceived women in sports journalism the same way as did the public. Male sports editors and reporters thought of their female colleagues as novelty items, who were not very serious about the profession and certainly did not possess the credentials of the men. Male sports journalists also felt threatened by their female counterparts, and to this day some still feel that female sports journalists are plucking jobs out of the male job pool. Of course, that isn't a new theme, regardless of which male-dominated industry one is discussing.

As a student at the University of Minnesota in 1962, Anne Gillespie-Lewis began writing for the *Minnesota Daily*, one of the largest college newspapers in the country at the time. One of her first assignments was a sports story, a women's sports story of course. Although claiming to have no ambition to be a sportswriter, Lewis continued to receive sports assignments and then began to request them. But even then Lewis received a taste of discrimination.

"They had one big newsroom, and a little separate room for sports,"

Lewis recalled. "The guy who was the sports editor would not let me come in that room. I had to write my sports stories, take it to the door, knock and hand it to him.

"He left at the end of the year, and the next guy who was sports editor actually let me in the room," Lewis went on. "Big deal! Gee, thanks!"

Lewis continued writing sports, but she also branched out into feature writing and front-page news. In her senior year she became the assistant sports editor and was assigned to cover the Golden Gopher hockey team, a significant assignment. Upon graduation, Lewis took a job as a general assignment reporter at a daily newspaper in Greenwich, Connecticut. She left after a year and returned to Minnesota where she applied for a job at the *Minneapolis Star*. With no general reporter positions available, Lewis asked the personnel manager, half on a lark, if they needed a woman sports-writer. Since they had previously discussed the novelty of such a position, she was hired immediately, without anyone ever questioning her knowl-edge of sports.

"A lot of women sportswriters now come into the profession because they love sports and they know it inside and out," Lewis said. "I hesitate to say this, but I simply did not know sports. It sounds like I wasn't serious, but I was in my own particular way. I just didn't know all the rules."

That was in 1967 and Lewis said, at the time, that there were three other female sportswriters in the entire country, one in Washington, D.C., one in Washington state, and one in Kansas City. This distinction had its ad-vantages and disadvantages.

"I look back on those days with a lot of fondness, in a lot of ways," Lewis said. "And yet I tolerated a lot of condescension. A lot of being patted on the head, a lot of hostility, even if it was somewhat veiled. Most of this didn't come from the athletes."

Lewis also became a prop for the marketing department. "I was a distinct oddity, and they promoted the heck out of me," Lewis said. "Because they knew a good thing when they saw it. They definitely did try to capitalize on the novelty of having a woman sportswriter. The promotion department . . . that is their job. But I must admit, I was in cahoots with the editors sometimes."

"The year after Peggy Fleming won the gold medal, she came to town with the Ice Follies. They sent me out to skate with her and interview her. They wanted a picture of the two of us, but they wanted me to fall. In Minnesota, everyone can skate, and we don't fall. I said I'm not going to do that. I'm not Peggy Fleming, but I can skate and I don't fall. They made me fall because it was cute and made more of a story."

Another feature story Lewis recalled was being asked to drive a dogsled through a park in the middle of downtown Minneapolis—not a small feat for someone who weighs 100 pounds. "The dogs got loose on me," Lewis chuckled. "I mean they were out of my control. And they had just told me that each of the dogs cost approximately $500. And they were heading for the busiest street in town with me hanging on by one arm. It was awful."

Between novelty stories, Lewis reported on high school and college football and basketball and, of course, women's sports, primarily gymnastics. Despite her determination and dedication to her job, Lewis still had a difficult time gaining favor with her fellow employees.

"I think it was more a sense they were shocked," Lewis explained. "They thought a woman should not do this. They were uneasy about me. No one was outright nasty to me, but they would ignore me, pretend I wasn't there. That sort of thing happened much more than outward abuse.

"It was very lonely because I had no one to talk to who did what I did," Lewis continued. "No one I knew anyway. Some of the guys were great to me and helped me a good deal more than they would have had to. I don't want to take anything away from them. It was mostly the older guys who were not fond of me."

Lewis worked for the *Star* for four years, three of them in sports. Writing for her hometown paper was advantageous from a readership standpoint, because Lewis does not recall receiving a lot of negative mail, although, in her words, she did receive "quite a bit of mail." Lewis also remembers being kept out of the locker rooms of the North Stars (National Hockey League) and the Twins (professional baseball). Most of her recollection, though, is positive. And her experiences give her an advantage many women would envy.

"It serves me right to have married an Englishman who knows cricket and nothing else. A few weeks ago he said, 'Now Annie, let me see. If the Vikings win the game tomorrow they go the Rose Bowl.' He was trying to be sociable. But I had to explain to him that the Vikings would never go to the Rose Bowl."

Despite the efforts of Lewis and other women in sports journalism over the years, most women, to this day, can't get away with the polite instruction Lewis gave her husband describing the difference between the University of Minnesota, who plays in the Big Ten Conference and, as a member, could qualify to go to the Rose Bowl, and the Vikings of the National Football League, who play for the opportunity to go to the Super Bowl.

An ESPN CHILTON sports poll released in July 1994 indicated that 80 percent of the respondents viewed the increase in women sportscasters in recent years as favorable. In fact, more men (81 percent) viewed the trend as positive than women (78 percent). More than 1,000 adults were polled over the telephone on the topic of women sportscasters from June 7 through July 4. When asked if they would like to see more women sportscasters, 67 percent responded yes. When asked if viewers are tougher on women sportscasters than on men sportscasters, however, 65 percent said they were tougher on women sportscasters, 10 percent claimed they treated both the same, and just 16 percent said they were tougher on men sportscasters.

"Now, with most viewers, I can mispronounce a name or something and it's no problem," said ESPN's Chris Berman. "But if one of the women did they are in deep shit. Rightly or wrongly. Some viewers might look at a woman sportscaster as guilty until proven innocent, and the males are innocent until proven guilty."

Despite the ESPN CHILTON poll, there is still a degree of acceptance for women sports journalists that comes through great pain, figuratively and literally. Considering the work of incredibly talented, knowledgeable women like ESPN's Robin Roberts and Lesley Visser, *Sports Illustrated*'s Sally Jenkins, Rachel Shuster of *USA Today*, ESPN Radio's Nanci Donnellan (a.k.a. the Fabulous Sports Babe), and others, it is difficult to comprehend the reluctance of the sporting society to see these professionals with gender blinders. Even though, as a society, we have conquered many of these types of mind-bending quandaries, the mail of disdain still flows.

"As I began to get a lot of people corresponding with me, they were telling me at every point if they disagreed with me," said Shuster. Shuster writes a column for *USA Today*'s sports section, among other duties. "Or if I happened to make a mistake, they would say you are just proving again what I have always thought, that women don't belong in sports. Or, why don't you go cover something like the women's page."

Some of Shuster's colleagues can relate to this mentality, fortunately some to a lesser degree of venom. "For women to be doing sports in the 1990s, that's not such a big deal," said ESPN's Roberts. "I think everyone has accepted it. But again, there's something different about sports. It's that last bastion of male bonding. You women can have everything else, your politics, your business, just leave us alone here."

Lesley Visser has been covering sports for twenty-three years, first as a writer for the *Boston Globe* for fourteen years, then as the NFL sideline reporter for CBS Sports, and now as a pro football reporter for ESPN. She has seen the public perception gradually change.

"I think there's an enormous difference [from when I started twenty years ago]," Visser said. "All to the positive. Twenty years ago, men insisted

sports was something a woman couldn't know or learn. I remember receiving letters at the *Globe* that said, basically, 'I'm not going to read anything you or any other broad writes.' When I listen to sports talk radio
shows, many of the men who call in don't know nearly as much as the
women I know in this business. But it's not perfect. There are still male
fans, coaches, and players who still feel we don't belong.''

Suzyn Waldman has been working at WFAN for more than ten years.
The FAN, New York City's sports talk radio station, is probably the premier all-sports talk station in the country. Waldman, who covers the Yankees and Knicks for the station, has accomplished some milestones in her
brief career. In the summer of 1993, she provided color commentary for a
few New York Mets broadcasts, and in July 1995 she became the first
woman to work a network broadcast of professional baseball, providing
commentary on the Texas Rangers–New York Yankees contest broadcast
on ABC and the Baseball Network.

Waldman grew up in Boston and was a diehard Red Sox fan. She had
her own season ticket to Fenway Park when she was three-and-a-half years
old. To her, the Yankees were like the bad cousins you see once a year at
Thanksgiving and fight with all the time. She loves baseball with a passion.
It comes second only to her first love, a fifteen-year stint as a Broadway
singer. She was also a devout Celtics fan and can recall attending many
games at the Boston Garden with her grandfather. Waldman views the
acceptance issue from two different perspectives.

"Fans were terrific," Waldman said of her commentary stint with the
Mets. "I had one awful letter from a woman, and I found that very interesting. I had one guy call WFAN and he said, 'This is nothing against you
Suzyn, but I just don't want anybody telling me about a pitch who doesn't
know what it feels like to hit a home run.'

"My comeback was, not only do you not know if I have ever hit a home
run or not, but Red Barber certainly didn't, Mel Allen certainly didn't.
And there are a whole lot of obstetricians in this country that now should
turn in their licenses because they certainly don't know what it's like to
have a baby."

For Waldman, the opportunity to do baseball commentary was also an
internal struggle. "I was very aware of the fact that if I messed this up,
someone else wasn't going to get a chance," Waldman recalled. "And it
went through my mind the whole time because then people can turn
around and say, 'Well if Suzyn Waldman can't do it, then no woman can.'

"It's not as if people were going to turn on the radio and say, 'Oh, who's
that?' Everybody knew what they were going to hear, and that was not a

concern to me. But I was real aware that if I made a mistake of any kind, someone was going to use it against somebody who is out there in the seventh grade."

Nanci Donnellan knows what the people think. And if she doesn't like it she hangs up on them. That's her prerogative. Donnellan has been the host of her own radio talk show for more than fifteen years. She has worked in Tampa, Boston, and Seattle, and recently she celebrated her first anniversary with ESPN Radio. Her show is known to be outrageous, fun, and, most of all, never boring. She won't hesitate to hang up on a caller or give one the "Geek of the Week" award, reserved for the worst call of the week. She can give you a lesson in "babeocracy" or send you an item from the "Babe Gear" apparel line. Also known as the Fabulous Sports Babe, Donnellan uses any negative perceptions to her advantage.

"I think it [positive perception] is a national thing," Donnellan said. "For example, I don't think people say, 'Oh, there's that woman.' They say, Suzyn is talking about the Yankees, or Robin [Roberts] or Linda [Cohn] is on SportsCenter.' I don't think they go through that gender thing.

"I'm sure there are going to be people who will never get it," Donnellan added. "But it's not like it was twenty years ago and it probably isn't like it was ten years ago. But I don't ever expect it to be OK with everybody because people are different. There are a lot of rednecks in the world . . . but I hang up on them and make a living off of those idiots."

One group of people Donnellan and her colleagues can't hang up on is their male coworkers. In addition to proving themselves worthy to a cynical, demanding spectating audience, women in the sports media must display their value to a skeptical male office pool, from the producers of their shows to the editors and their fellow writers in the newsroom.

"The problem with women in this medium is your colleagues pure and simple," said WFAN's Waldman. "The people that hire, the people that you work with. They don't want you there, that's the bottom line. I've said this before and it's not going to surprise anybody. That is where the problem is. There isn't a man in that station who doesn't think he knows more than I do, no matter what it is. I don't care if it is a twenty-year-old or a sixty-year-old. There is no one who believes I know more than they do on any subject. That's a problem."

ESPN's Roberts has a more comical take on that topic. "I have a mug that says on it, 'Whatever a woman does, she has to do twice as well as a man to be considered half as good. Luckily, this is not that difficult.'

"This is a mug I bring out to my set every night. And the guys are not trying to be ugly or anything like that. I don't want to say twice as much work, necessarily. It does seem double the amount that you put in to be able to get a certain assignment. It has to be justified double before you are considered to do something.

"It's a bat of an eye to send somebody to do the Final Four or the Super Bowl. But if a woman asked for that assignment, they'd say, 'Whoa, let me think about it, let's see all of the ramifications.' And that's unfortunate."

Prior to *USA Today*, Shuster had worked at the *Washington Star* and a daily newspaper in Albany, New York. While Shuster firmly believes her male colleagues at the *Star* and *USA Today* are supportive of her efforts, her experience in Albany was nothing short of brutal. Shuster went to Albany from Washington, D.C., and became the first woman ever hired at the sports section at that paper. To add to her dilemma, she was assigned the minor league hockey beat, the epitome of sports for the people in that region.

"I did have trouble with men in my department there because they were questioning my credibility," Shuster recalled. "They were not terribly supportive. Part of that, also, was I was coming from D.C. and was perceived, rightly or wrongly, as having a chip on my shoulder."

In addition to covering the team, Shuster was assigned a hockey column, which seemed to compound the situation. "Unfortunately, I was coming in at the same time as a new coach," Shuster said. "The general manager was a long-standing citizen in the Glen Falls–Albany community. It just so happened, in my column, I ended up taking the side of the coach instead of the general manager on the issues.

"The whole notion of a woman covering hockey, coming from outside Albany, was apparently too much to take," Shuster continued. "The situation got very nasty."

Jody Goldstein, who writes for the *Houston Chronicle*, covers a little bit of everything: Houston Astros baseball, Houston Oilers football, Rice University athletics, and women's professional tennis. Goldstein has a unique perspective.

"One of the big differences is that men don't rub off on each other," Goldstein explained. "If a man does something idiotic, it reflects on him and him only. Unfortunately, if a woman mishandles herself, it still reflects on *all* other women. Which shouldn't be the case, but absolutely is the case."

Goldstein remembered vividly such an encounter while covering the Oilers. Goldstein and the rest of the beat reporters were waiting to get into the locker room after the game, and the morning crew from a local radio station showed up to produce what Goldstein called a fluff piece. According to Goldstein, the buxom female host of this morning show was dressed in a low-cut halter top and a tight leather miniskirt and was standing outside the locker room giggling and acting . . . well, immature would be appropriate. Goldstein's female colleague from the rival *Houston Post* stepped in.

"She pulled this radio reporter aside and said, 'You don't act like that, you don't dress like that. What you do reflects on me and I am too much of a professional . . . ' She really let her have it. I couldn't believe she actually did what she did. But we were all thinking it. And what she said is true. You work so hard to build up your own reputation and someone like that can come along and ruin it for everyone."

All of these women, however, did say that they had been assisted and supported by many male colleagues along the way. In fact, some insist their male colleagues have helped their careers substantially. Even if it seems like a small deed, it can play a tremendous part in a person's career.

Visser received that kind of boost early in her career at the *Boston Globe*. "My experiences have been very positive," Visser said. "The *Globe* was a very progressive newspaper. I went there in the summer of Watergate and they gave me tremendous assignments, that honestly, I didn't deserve. I had only covered Massachusetts high school football at the lowest classification.

"In 1976 I was the first woman to cover the NFL [National Football League] as a beat," Visser continued. "Some people could have made it very difficult for me. Will McDonough [then with the *Globe*, now with NBC Sports] was very supportive of me. He called the Patriots coaches and management and told them to give me a chance because I was a hard worker and I would do a good job."

As far as working twice as hard as her male colleagues, Visser doesn't hold that sentiment. "One misconception is that women work harder than men. I would find it hard to believe that anyone works harder than John Madden, for example. I tried to do two things [when I got started]. I was very cautious about being professional around the players. And I tried to do things with the other writers. We played pickup basketball, we went out for pizzas. I just wanted to be thought of as a *Globe* staff writer, not the *woman* sportswriter. By the time I went to CBS, they could see I already knew the players and the coaches."

Roberts believes that the man who helped her gain public acceptance when she went to ESPN is one of her fellow hosts. "The person I work with the most is Chris Berman," Roberts explained. "And I give him a lot of credit because he set the tone for how other people have accepted me. Because he always accepted me as an equal. He was never condescending to me, he never talked down to me or made me feel anything less than equal. And when viewers at home see that, they say, 'If she's okay with Chris, then she's okay with me.' He really helped set the tone."

Berman has been lauded by other women in the industry for being supportive of their efforts. The Brown University graduate is humble about the praise. "I think they [the women] overstate it," Berman said. "Here's what I recognize, male or female. Do they know what they are talking about? Do they love what they are doing? Are they enthusiastic? I don't know if that separates me from many people. It should not.

"Robin [Roberts] you could see, right away, this is someone who knew what she's doing, who loves what she's doing because it's fun. She's classy, and she's a terrific person, someone you would want to be friends with even if you didn't work together. She's the complete package. Is it a conscious thing on my part? No, I wouldn't give myself that much credit. I just give everyone the benefit of the doubt out of the box."

Berman, who is best known for his propensity to aptly apply nifty nicknames to professional athletes, believes there is more to this issue than the surface arguments. "The trouble that women have, probably not too many of them went out and had a catch with their dad when they were seven years old," Berman mused. "That's not their fault. But there's a part of sports that hits the majority of guys that doesn't hit the majority of women. That being said, the pool of guys that, quote, 'get it' is going to be bigger than the pool of women who, quote, 'get it.'

"There are some, Gayle [Gardner formerly of NBC], Robin, Lesley Visser. They get it. They come across, they have a point of view that I don't have. I am always interested in someone's point of view who understands it. And it doesn't have to be my point of view. They may look at things a little differently than I do. And that's good. There are some guys I work with who don't really get it."

Another way women in the sports media have strengthened their place in the industry is through the formation of the Association for Women in the Sports Media (AWSM). Started nearly ten years ago, the association comprises sports reporters, sports editors, and radio and television personnel. The membership numbers more than 500. The organization gives women in the industry a collective voice, and it has grown in strength over the last three years.

Now with its own treasury, the AWSM offers three annual scholarships for young women in broadcasting, copy editing, and sports reporting. At its annual convention, the group has a job fair that attracts sports editors searching to diversify their staff, and the convention itself gives the organization's members an opportunity to address issues that might not be approachable on an individual basis. Cathy Henkel, the sports editor at the *Seattle Times*, has been president of AWSM.

"I think just by organizing a group and getting a voice is important," Henkel explained. "People listen to a bigger voice when individuals band together. I think we have the support of the sports editors in the country. They understand it is important to diversify their staffs. They are hearing that, not only from us, but from their managing editors and owners.

"The next spot is how do you get that way [diverse]?" Henkel said. "I think we can help in terms of providing candidates for jobs and making sure that we know names to offer when a sports editor job comes open. We are trying to gather a job bank, because, in the scheme of things, there aren't very many [women in the sports media]."

Henkel estimates that only approximately 10 percent of all sports journalists in the United States are women. That's counting everyone from Robin Roberts down to the newest rookie. According to Henkel, there are only six female sports editors at large daily newspapers across the country.

Unfortunately for Gayle Gardner, nothing could halt her departure from NBC Sports. Gardner started at ESPN in the early years as a SportsCenter anchor and took advantage of her talents and abilities and made the move to NBC in 1988. Gardner, first a reporter and writer, was a studio host for football, basketball, and the Olympics. But in the late fall of 1993, Gardner became a free agent with no teams bidding for her services. Gardner left NBC under questionable circumstances, just after the network hired Hannah Storm. Women in the industry believe Gardner's fate was the product of the network female quota system.

Not until the emergence of Gardner, ESPN's Roberts and Visser, and Andrea Joyce at CBS have women enjoyed substantial assignments in television sports. Perhaps because of the Phyllis George–Jayne Kennedy stereotype, or perhaps just because of the old boys' network, it took network television a long time to provide a woman with the opportunity to contribute to a sports show in a meaningful manner. The party line among network sports executives had always been the theme that they were broadcasting to a predominantly male audience. They couldn't, therefore, justify having a woman tell Joe Six-pack what to do on third down and seven yards to go when the defense is mounting an all-out blitz. "That is like the theory that you can't write about murder unless you go and commit murder," said Henkel. Her organization dispelled that myth by conducting an interest survey that showed that nearly 40 percent of the readers of the sports pages are women.

Still, Gardner's departure shows that, in the 1990s, the networks still subscribe to the "I got my one, who've you got" syndrome. Some women in the industry believe Gardner should have updated her resumé at the slightest hint NBC was hiring another woman in sports.

"I am horrified at how she was treated and what has happened to her," said WFAN's Waldman. "I just thought she was a fabulous role model for everybody. I remember her back in Boston when she went on the air. There were women who had done it before, but when Gayle went on the air, she was the first person who really didn't make mistakes, she knew what she was doing.

"Lesley [Visser] is one of my closest friends and we talk about this all the time. Lesley is much less cynical than I am, but I look around and I've said flat out, if you are a woman working full time at a network and you see another woman walk in the door, you better turn around and get going. One of you is not going to be around long. Lesley keeps telling me it's getting better. It's not getting better because the fact is women are not allowed to be anything but *the woman*."

One source, requesting anonymity, added more substance to the case. "I know through the grapevine I heard from twenty different people that certain people at NBC didn't like Gayle and loved Hannah. They were going to do everything they could to make life miserable for Gayle. I think it's pretty accurate. It's an unsaid thing. You can't prove it, but it exists."

Because of her talent and experience, ESPN's Roberts is a likely candidate for a network slot in the future. Gardner was at ESPN when Roberts started in Bristol, Connecticut, in 1990. Although she believes that the network quota system has been in place for a number of years, she thinks it might be evolving in a positive nature.

"At every network, when one woman leaves, she is replaced by a woman," Roberts said. "We heard when Hannah was hired, that was it for Gayle. I was personally offended by people saying to me, 'Well I guess you can't go to NBC now, they just hired Hannah.' I said I didn't want that job anyway, I want Bob Costas's job. That's a joke. But that's how I felt.

"I think the networks are starting to get away from that syndrome," Roberts continued. "You are beginning to see two and three women at a network and that is real progress. But I was saddened by the case at NBC."

Gaining acceptance from your readership or viewership, as well as from your colleagues, is critical to any profession, perhaps none more so than the sports media. Equally paramount to the task is the cooperation, respect, and approval of those people most critical to executing that job—the coaches and athletes of the teams that are covered.

All Lisa Olson was looking for in September 1990 was her weekly feature story on the New England Patriots of the NFL. Olson, then twenty-six, was a sportswriter for the *Boston Herald* and covered the Patriots for the paper on a regular basis. While interviewing Maurice Hurst in the locker room after a practice, a number of naked Patriots players crowded around Olson making lewd comments and gestures. Olson left the locker room without finishing her interview with Hurst. Olson claimed that this was sexual harassment at its worst; she also asserted that it was orchestrated.[1]

Olson eventually left the *Herald* and went to another newspaper—in Australia. What was worse than the treatment Olson received from the players were the actions of the Patriots owner, Victor Kiam II, and various fans after the incident. Kiam, the Remington shaver mogul, said after the incident that he couldn't disagree with his players' actions and that the *Herald* was asking for trouble by assigning a female reporter to his team. He also made other unfounded accusations that he later retracted. After the incident was made public, Olson was again covering the Patriots at a home game. While she was making her way toward the locker room with other reporters after the game, the crowd began chanting obscenities at Olson.[2]

Kiam later took out more than $100,000 worth of newspaper advertisements claiming innocence and apologizing to Olson. He also had a lengthy discussion with Olson, but later spoiled all of that by allegedly making a "Lisa Olson" joke at a charitable dinner where he was speaking. The joke, of course, got an uproarious response from the guests.[3]

One Patriots player was fined a meager $2,000 by the league, but some believe that he never paid the fine. That same season, Sam Wyche, then head coach of the Cincinnati Bengals, was also disciplined by the league for keeping a woman reporter away from his locker room. The NFL created an equal access policy for journalists in 1985.

Developing a news story contains a number of elements. One is required not only to detail the action of the contest, pinpoint the critical moments, and evaluate the outcome, but also to portray the emotions of the participants. In order to do the latter, a reporter must often venture into the locker room after the game to catch the coaches and athletes in the heat of the moment. Nothing adds the right flavor to a story more than an angry or jubilant athlete or coach who has just left the arena. If, as some have hinted, athletics is the last male bastion, then the locker room is the shrine. And the unwritten sign at the doorway is clearly written. No women allowed.

"We are going into a place that's considered an inner sanctum," related Henkel. "The perception is you are judging their performance, and they also think you are judging their body. Which, of course, you aren't doing.

But that's what men do, and they think women do the same. They don't understand there's a difference. In any other kind of business, you don't enter that kind of intimate atmosphere unless you are a professional, like a doctor or a dentist. It is an obstacle that doesn't exist anywhere else in the world or in any other career."

While policies and procedures have changed in order to improve access for women, the prevailing sentiment of players and coaches, nonetheless, remains vehemently opposed. Despite the necessity to get the story, some women in the business understand this attitude.

"You don't interview President Clinton in his bathroom to ask him policy on the nation," ESPN's Roberts said. "Why should we go into the locker room? I don't know of any athlete who likes a man or a woman in that locker room. My fight is not about equal access to the locker room, my fight is about equal access to the player. The player just happens to be in the locker room. There's a big difference there."

Visser believes the whole issue is blown out of proportion. "Ninety-eight to 99 percent of the time nothing happens, but that doesn't get reported," the ESPN reporter said. "You don't hear, '500 female reporters went into the locker room today and nothing happened.' I get a lot of phone calls and letters from students who want to interview me for their term papers, and I tell them I am only going to talk about the locker room for 3 percent of the time because it's only 3 percent of my job.

"It's a place of business, we're not going into their homes," Visser continued. "Most athletes treat you how you treat them. The biggest misunderstanding is that nobody has to be naked! There is a cooling off period before the media can go into the locker room. The coaches and players can get their thoughts and composure together, get a shower, and get changed. This isn't some Chippendale's thing."

Still, the fact remains that occasionally incidents do occur to verify the axiom. While some female reporters claim they have never had a horrifying experience, it seems each has a let-me-tell-you incident to tell. Some are less spectacular than others. WFAN's Waldman thinks there's an unwritten formula.

"There are three stages every woman in the sports media goes through," Waldman said. "First you get laughed at, second you get viciously attacked, and the third stage is acceptance when they figure out you're not all that bad. Every woman in the sports media has an athlete and an event. An athlete who has gotten them through something and an event to turn it around."

Waldman's athlete and event both occurred in one instance. During her first year on the Yankee beat in 1987, the Toronto Blue Jays were in town. George Bell, then a feared slugger in the American League and one of the offensive leaders of the Blue Jays, refused to speak to the New York media that season because he felt that the New York writers had cost him the Most Valuable Player award the previous season.

"Toronto was a very bad clubhouse to deal with in that time," Waldman recalled. "The last trip in, it was late September, I was interviewing another player and I saw reporters start walking over toward Bell. And I thought, if he is going to talk I better get over there. He saw me coming and started screaming just awful obscenities. He kept throwing towels at me, it was the most vile thing. Not a player moved, not a writer moved. I'm thinking why isn't anybody helping me here?

"I thought, just let me get out of here before I start to cry," Waldman said. "Then I heard someone say, 'What's her name?' And somebody answered, 'Suzyn something.' And I heard, 'Suzyn,' and I turned around and it was Jesse Barfield. And he said, 'I went three-for-four today, don't you want to talk to me?' It was the single nicest act of kindness. I had never met him before. I marched right back in there. Then the other reporters started to come over toward Jesse, and he told them, 'No, you go back and talk to George Bell.' It was amazing and it was a great thing to do in front of [his] teammates."

Roberts recalls being confronted and withheld from the University of Georgia locker room in 1989 after the Southeastern Conference men's basketball championship while she was working for a network affiliate in Atlanta. USA Today's Shuster tells of the time a Green Bay Packer fondled himself in front of her while she was conducting an interview, and she also remembers being pinched and hollered at. ESPN Radio's Donnellan was kept out of locker rooms when she was covering the Tampa Bay Buccaneers in the mid–1980s even though the NFL had an open-door policy. Though not a required task now compared to her days as a reporter and a stringer for CBS, Donnellan gets steamed just thinking about the subject.

"Who in the world wants to be in one of those?" asked Donnellan. "I don't think anyone wants to, but that is the venue and you can't tell me that I can't run in there to get a quote solely based on the fact that I am a woman. That is my job, that is how I make my living. You are asking me to not be able to make a living.

"If you are an official and you are watching ESPN, you see ESPN's lead NFL person is Andrea Kremer," Donnellan continued. "It has got to register somewhere that you have got to stop trying to do that because you might accidentally do it to Andrea Kremer. So even the dumbest person in the world has got to get it by now."

Leave it to Berman to provide the male perspective. "We all grew up in the 1960s and 1970s and we think, hey come on in," Berman mused. "But if you're a guy, you're still uncomfortable with women in the locker room. Since you were in grammar school, you changed in separate locker rooms than the females. Now, the female reporters are not changing with you, but it's something that deep down you are not used to. This is something that's instilled in you when you're seven, eight, nine years old. So you would have to be a veteran [player] of fifteen years to make a wash. I'm not trying to be funny. It's ingrained."

Always the optimist, Visser can point to a personal experience that proves that players and coaches are more accepting. In June 1993, while jogging in Central Park, Visser fell and dislocated and badly fractured her hip. While she was in Lenox Hill Hospital in New York, Visser received hundreds of flowers, cards, and gifts from players, coaches, and entire organizations. Well-wishers included the Dallas Cowboys, Chicago Bulls, New York Jets, Indianapolis Colts, Fox's John Madden, Terry Bradshaw, and Jimmy Johnson (none of whom were with Fox at the time), NFL commissioner Paul Tagliabue, Tampa Bay Buccaneer coach Sam Wyche, Kentucky men's basketball coach Rick Pitino, and Louisiana State men's basketball coach Dale Brown.

Considering Visser's attitude and talent, it is no wonder she ended up at ESPN before the 1994 NFL season. The Total Sports Network is the most progressive and female friendly of the major television entities—from the very beginning, when Gardner was a regular on SportsCenter, to the present, when a plethora of females are given ample opportunity to carry out significant assignments on a daily basis.

While Gardner got things started in Bristol, many others have carried on the tradition of quality. Roberts, Visser, Andrea Kremer, and SportsCenter anchor Linda Cohn are the more recognizable names. Sharlene Hawkes has been with the station since 1987 and has filled a variety of roles, from sideline reporter on college football, to "Scholastic Sports America," to hosting the ESPN "Fitness Club." ESPN2 "SportsNight" anchor Suzy Kolber, ESPN2 "SportSmash" anchor Deb Kaufman, and the Fabulous Sports Babe on ESPN Radio round out a deep and talented group.

"I think long before I got here in 1988 the company had a history of being aggressive and saw there were advantages for putting a diversity of talent, whether minorities or women, on the air," said ESPN Executive Editor John Walsh.

"My personal history has been the same way. I'd always thought the women's perspective in sports was a healthy antidote to the locker room mentality that can develop. I think it's good we get a different perspective, a good sense of detail."

As executive editor, Walsh is responsible for all news and information on the network. He supervises all the coverage, news reports, and news shows, such as "SportsCenter," "NFL Gameday," and "Baseball Tonight," and such issue-oriented shows as "Outside the Lines" and "UpClose." He also supervises news and information for the radio side. Finally, Walsh is responsible for personnel. He believes that a conscious effort is made at ESPN to consider women when positions become available.

"Absolutely, we try to identify qualified women and we try to encourage them," Walsh stated. "I think in an environment that has been male-dominated, the enlightened workplace of the 1990s is diverse. We spend time identifying talent we like, even if we don't have any openings. We will bring them in for an interview and ask them to stay in touch. When an opening becomes available, we are in a position to hire a quality individual."

Berman has been at the station since its third week of existence, and he has worked with many of the women who have come through Bristol. Many women have given him credit for being very supportive of their work.

"This is a unique place," Berman explained. "There's always been room on staff for everybody. We've always been enlightened from day one. Knowledge, enthusiasm, and ability to communicate have always been viewed as important. We've always had so much to do we don't have a lot of ego problems. There's time for everybody. We have a nice system built in. Women can prosper and be noticed. At the other networks, they don't have as much room, the ceiling isn't as high."

The key for ESPN is that it hires qualified women. It doesn't necessarily place someone on the air because of beauty pageant credentials or physical appearance. These women have substance, and they display that characteristic in their work.

Kremer, the Chicago-based correspondent for "NFL Gameday," contributes to other shows as well. She joined the network in 1989 and has covered all the major sporting events, from the Super Bowl to the National Basketball Association championship. Prior to joining ESPN, Kremer worked at NFL Films for six years as a producer and director. She also contributed as a reporter for "This is the NFL," the nationally syndicated radio show produced by NFL Films. The cum laude graduate from the University of Pennsylvania received an Emmy nomination in 1986 for writing and editing "Autumn Ritual."

Cohn previously covered the Seattle Mariners, Seahawks, and Supersonics along with University of Washington football for KIRO-TV in Seattle. She was the first full-time female sports anchor on a national radio show when she hosted for ABC Radio Network and WABC TalkRadio for three years. This former member of the boys' ice hockey team at Newfield (New York) High School also did some work at WFAN in New York.

"We are intimidating because we are the sports experts," Walsh said. "Women really have to know their stuff. People will accept them. It's a challenge. The networks are considered the big leagues by many people. When we hired Lesley [Visser], Lesley said, 'Now I'm going to the big leagues.' We place more emphasis on nuts and bolts, meat and potatoes. If you don't have that kind of background, your credibility is challenged."

While all of the women at ESPN have had tremendous success, perhaps none has flourished as much as Roberts. She has become a prime time player as evidenced by her recent signing of a multiyear, big-bucks contract. She anchors "SportsCenter," has been on "NFL Prime Time" and "Outside the Lines," and she has done play-by-play commentary for women's tennis and basketball. She has covered and been a commentator for a variety of events, such as the NFL draft, the Final Four, the Summer Olympics, and Wimbledon.

Roberts was a sports reporter and anchor for WAGA-TV in Atlanta before she joined ESPN. She also served similar roles at WSMV-TV in Nashville, WLOX-TV in Biloxi, Mississippi, and WDAM-TV in Hattiesburg, Mississippi. She has received numerous awards, including the 1993 Excellence in Sports Journalism award from the Northeastern University Center for the Study of Sport in Society. Roberts graduated cum laude from Southeastern Louisiana University and was an outstanding player for the Lady Lions basketball squad. She is the third all-time leading scorer and rebounder in school history and one of only three players to have accumulated more than 1,000 points and 1,000 rebounds in a career.

"The main reason I re-signed with ESPN is the opportunities," Roberts said. "I am doing play-by-play for college basketball, I have the studio show, NFL, the French Open, Wimbledon. There's so many different things I am doing.

"I'm a kid in a candy store," Roberts continued. "I am a sports journalist, yes, but I am a sports fanatic. I'm a very blessed individual and I am having fun because I'm doing what it is I wanted to do with my life. How many people can say that? I'm having a good time and smiling because I know that I've beaten the odds."

Walsh, who has an impressive resumé as well, isn't surprised by Roberts's success. Having worked at *Newsday*, *Rolling Stone*, the *Washington Post*, *Newsweek*, *U.S. News & World Report*, and being the founding editor of *Inside Sports* magazine, the former journalism professor at the University of Missouri knows quality work. "Robin is a tremendous leader," Walsh said. "She takes the role well, she's responsible, she's mature, and she's an inspiration to the people who work with her."

Considering the high caliber of women in the industry, young girls have an outstanding, albeit small, core of role models. Young girls who aspire to one day be the next Robin Roberts or Lesley Visser need to study the careers of all these women. These women are at this place in their careers because they worked their way up the proverbial ladder. They started their careers covering high school football and basketball and continued to work and dream. Most reporters have diverse backgrounds founded in a variety of disciplines. And, as Berman alluded, they are excited about their work, and that feature is evident in their work.

"Women in this industry have made great leaps and bounds," Roberts said. "We have done tremendous work in the last decade and I'm very excited to be involved in that movement. I am by no means content. I work with a gentleman on Sunday mornings, Dick Schaap, whom I admire a great deal, who has grey hair. My hope is that I will be allowed to have grey hair and still be on television doing the sports.

"I long for the day when I am interviewed and it will have nothing to do with gender," Roberts concluded. "But deep in my heart, I don't feel that will ever be the case. I think it will always be an issue. Maybe not as big as it is now or has been. But as long as sports remains an obsession in American culture and world culture, gender will be an issue. One that women will have to accept and be able to go on from there."

9

Where Do We Go from Here?

Fathers are leading the charge, most organizations will tell you that. Mothers don't have to do it anymore because fathers want their daughters to get an equal shot. That's what's going to change things. Fathers and brothers who see women as their daughters and sisters, not as some woman who is going to take their job or threaten their masculinity.

—Cathy Henkel, sports editor,
Seattle Times

The rhetoric is continually exchanged, and the battle lines are clearly and firmly entrenched, but the question remains, "Why?" It is not easy to change decades of certain habits, behavior, and ideas. It is possible, however. Sometimes it's difficult to embrace the realities and envision the possibilities. But, as the Nike commercials say, "Just Do It."

Jim Haluck is not the most popular high school athletic director in Anne Arundel County, Maryland. Haluck took over as athletic director at South River Senior High School in Edgewater in 1989 after serving as a junior varsity coach in both soccer and lacrosse. His experiences as a junior varsity coach dictated his initial plan of action.

"As a junior varsity coach, you didn't get anything, you had to beg for a couple rolls of tape," Haluck explained. "It didn't need to be that way. When I took over, the first thing I did was evaluate what everybody had. I set a goal to get everyone, boys and girls, up to snuff. We upgraded the essential things first, like equipment and uniforms. Then we said, 'We need facilities.' "

For their efforts, Haluck, his staff, and school were honored with *Athletic Management* magazine's Excellence in Equity Award for 1995.

In the last four to five years, South River has built a second stadium, redone their time schedules so that the boys' and girls' teams share the prime time night games, and purchased new uniforms for the boys' and girls' varsity teams. Dugouts have been added to both the softball and baseball fields, and both have also been fenced in. New scoreboards have been added in the gymnasium as well as to the main stadium. The nonfootball stadium scoreboard now can accommodate up to ninety minutes, which is appropriate for soccer and lacrosse. A sprinkler system has been added to the second stadium as well, and Haluck would like to add sprinkler systems to the practice fields in the future. Haluck said that his department attempts to schedule an equal number of prime time games on the stadium field for both the boys' and girls' teams in comparable sports. The county was coming in the spring of 1996 to construct a new field hockey field for South River, complete with a special short grass to make the field hockey ball travel smoothly.

The biggest change, and most monumental in the eyes of Haluck's peers in the county, was changing the scheduling of girls' and boys' basketball. Now, the boys' and girls' teams alternate for the prime time 7:00 P.M. game and the less glamorous 5:00 P.M. contest. This item was one of the specific areas for which South River was awarded.

"It was difficult because scheduling is done countywide," Haluck said. "Our schedule changes affected the other county schools, because it changed the times of their boys' varsity games. It also changed the locations of the junior varsity games, so our efforts really affected two teams from the other schools."

The other schools have made a point to make Haluck aware of their displeasure—not very often verbally, but in their actions. According to Haluck, the South River boys' varsity team plays more 5:00 P.M. games than any other team in the twelve-team county. Haluck schedules from eighteen to twenty games per season, so some games must also be played against teams from outside Anne Arundel County. The South River players aren't always pleased with the schedule changes either.

"It bothers the kids more playing the 5:00 game," Haluck said. "Because they know they are not the highlight team. They know it's fair, but they don't always like it. The teams are very supportive of each other. If anyone catches any grief from the kids, it's usually directed to me.

"The girls have found out that it's not always so glamorous to play at night," Haluck explained. "Sometimes the field is damp from the dew and the grass is a little slick, and later in the fall it can get pretty cold after the sun goes down. But that has benefited our girls' teams for the playoffs, because they are used to those conditions now."

These efforts take proper planning as well as a commitment of resources. South River has made sure of both. Haluck has an athletic council that is made up of Haluck, his assistant athletic director, the head of the physical education department, and a faculty member who serves as the athletic administrator. Although the group is Haluck's sounding board, it also plays an important role in making major decisions.

South River has received donations of time and equipment from some companies to aid in facilities improvements, but a good deal of the necessary resources have come through the hard work of the school's booster club. According to Haluck, the school keeps two-thirds of its gate receipts, and the booster club generates additional revenue through food sales at athletic contests as well as through a variety of fund-raisers. Haluck estimates the booster club generates an average of $20,000 per year.

"Other schools in the county have looked at our efforts as a threat," Haluck said. "At county meetings, I have people from other schools tell me they are going to wait until the courts make them do it. That's silly. The courts don't care about athletics, they only care about legalities.

"I've told them to just try it, try it for two games," Haluck continued. "Two other schools in the county are rescheduling their games, and the world hasn't come to an end. What we do is we pick our rivals for each team, boys' and girls', and we schedule the rival as the prime time game. The rivals generate the most fan interest and that way we don't get hurt in gate receipts. You don't want to move too fast, and you must be careful what you do. We are showing it [equity] can be done."

An institution that is showing that gender equity can be successfully achieved at another level is Stanford University. Prior to the 1993–1994 academic year, Stanford unveiled a multimillion dollar Women's Sports Enhancement program. In four years, the athletic department's goal was to have 45 percent of its student-athletes be women. Three women's varsity sports teams were to be added, one a year through 1996–1997. Synchronized swimming, lacrosse, and water polo will be added to a Cardinal program that already is the leader in women's sports offerings. The added sports will bring the proportion of student-athletes in line as well as increase scholarships for women student-athletes by 29, from 73 to 102. Those additional scholarships will be spread among all of the women's teams, though, not just the three new teams.

The university planned to expand office facilities and locker rooms, added a softball field, increased tutoring, added medical and training facilities, and expanded publicity. Financial resources will come from aggressive fund-raising, revenue from the 1994 World Cup soccer matches, and increased revenue from football attendance. The department also hoped to increase the profitability of its women's teams.

This action plan was developed through the work of a small committee of four people. Cheryl L. Levick, the senior women's administrator in the department, was part of that committee along with the university's legal counsel, the faculty athletic representative, and the university's affirmative action officer. The committee analyzed the Cardinal athletic department through a voluntary Title IX review and ran the department through all thirteen checks in the Title IX test. They then brought in an outside agency to conduct interviews of student-athletes and coaches, and that agency then forwarded the independent study to the committee. The committee evaluated the independent study as well as its own work and was able to identify the shortcomings in the women's program. The three-year plan was developed from this thorough research process and, according to Levick, was redrafted about fifteen times before it was forwarded for presidential approval.

The two largest issues were the scholarships offered and the facilities. Offering twenty-nine more scholarships will address that shortage, and the university completed a new athletic building in December 1993 that addressed the need for locker rooms, strength and conditioning areas, sports medicine, and office space for the coaching staff. Externally, there was no softball facility comparable to the Cardinal national championship baseball complex, but plans were to have that structure built before the three-year plan concluded.

"We have been very proactive in this, and we are fortunate to have a very strong donor base that can help us raise the money required," Levick said. "We are totally self-funded; the university does not supplement our athletic programs at all. The income comes from gate receipts, television, our golf course, and fund-raising.

"We have a very strong commitment from the university to maintain a broad-based program," Levick continued. "We have 6,000 undergraduate students and approximately 15 percent are involved in intercollegiate athletics and another 10 percent are involved in club and intramural sports. By the end of the third year, we will offer equitable opportunities for our male and female athletes. We will be able to add to our women's program without diluting our men's program. It's the right thing to do and the fair thing to do."

Stanford is certainly in an enviable position. The Cardinal are annual contenders for national championships in a variety of sports. In 1991 Stanford captured national championships in five different sports. Its women's teams are particularly strong in basketball, volleyball, swimming, and diving.

Some will argue that Stanford is in a unique situation because of its ability to raise athletic funding through its donor base. Perhaps Stanford alumni have a greater proportion of disposable income to donate, but the notion that Stanford's donor base is better than everybody else's is not the point. The key is the manner in which Stanford is allocating those resources to improve its women's program. Money seems to be the prevailing factor in collegiate athletics, and it is one of the focal points for the continued progress of the gender equity.

"I am seeing a plateau of resources that are being added, and that troubles me," Levick said. "It goes along with the budgetary problems that we are seeing on the collegiate level. I hope we can get past this and continue moving upward. But I think we are stuck for a while. Until we can get past some of the financial problems we are seeing and resolve some of the litigation in the courts."

Dorothy McIntyre of the Minnesota State High School League summed it up most appropriately. "There is no finish line in gender equity. This is an ongoing road race that we face every single day. And if we believe in kids and we believe in equality in our society, then we welcome that opportunity to keep life fair for kids. Because if they don't experience it in the schools, how will they ever expect to understand how it will be when they are adults in our society?"

Notes

1. STILL STRUGGLING

1. *The Chronicle of Higher Education*, 9 April 1992.

2. National Collegiate Athletic Association, *Gender Equity Study* (Overland Park, KS: NCAA, 1990).

3. National Collegiate Athletic Association, *Gender Equity Study* (Overland Park, KS: NCAA, 1992).

4. Linda Jean Carpenter and Vivian R. Acosta, "Job Status: Reflections of Immobility and Resistance to Job Change among Senior Women Athletic Personnel" (Brooklyn College, 1992).

5. Ibid.

6. Warren Kalbacker, "20 Questions," *Playboy*, February 1994, 133.

7. Donna Lopiano, "Stop the Rhetoric: Daughters Deserve What the Law Requires," *USA Today*, 2 July 1993, 12C.

8. Women's Sports Foundation, "Miller Lite Report on Sports and Fitness in the Lives of Working Women," (Miller Brewing Company, Milwaukee, WI, 8 March 1993), 4.

9. Ibid.

10. Ibid., 9.

11. Rene Stutzman, "Sports Marketers Court Ladies," *York Daily Record* (PA), 13 October 1994, D1.

12. Associated Press, "California Woman Outstanding in Collegiate Pitching Debut," *Morristown Daily Record* (NJ), 17 February 1994, C2.

13. Karen Allen, "U.S. Men Want Their Share," *USA Today*, 10 February 1994, 12.

14. Greg Boeck, "O'Malley Succeeds with Bullets Even as Team Struggles," *USA Today*, 9 December 1993, 10C.

15. Bruce Horovitz, "Women Stir America's Cup Ads," *USA Today*, 16 March 1995, B1.

16. John Rowe, "These Women Play Hardball," *The Record* (Hackensack, NJ), 7 March 1994, S1.

17. Anita Manning, "Erasing Sexism from the Sports Rule Book," *USA Today*, 6 July 1994, 2D.

2. CALLING ALL DADS

1. Mark Scolforo, "All She Wants to Do Is Play Ball," *York Dispatch* (PA), 6 April 1995, E1.

2. Ibid.

3. Ibid.

4. Valerie T. Swain, "Sarah Just Wants Chance to Play Baseball," *York Daily Record* (PA), 6 April 1995, 1A.

5. Ibid.

6. Scolforo, "All She Wants," E1.

7. Ibid., E2.

8. Dan Fink, "Club Says Baseball 'for Boys,' " *York Daily Record* (PA), 10 April 1995, A1.

9. Barb Krebs, "Baseball: Delta Girl Strikes Out," *York Disptach* (PA), 10 April 1995, C1.

10. Kelly P. Kissel, "Female Coach Makes History," *Morristown Daily Record* (NJ), 24 August 1993, B4.

11. Nat Newell, "In a League of Her Own," *Anderson Independent-Mail* (SC), 1 July 1995, 1D, 5D.

12. New World Decisions, "Miller Lite Report on Women in Sports," (Miller Brewing Company, Milwaukee, WI, December 1985), 9.

13. Diagnostic Research, Inc., "The Wilson Report: Moms, Dads, Daughters and Sports," (Wilson Sporting Goods, Co. River Grove, IL, 7 June 1988), 29.

14. Women's Sports Foundation, "Miller Lite Report on Sports and Fitness in the Lives of Working Women," (Miller Brewing Company, Milwaukee, WI, 8 March 1993), 5.

15. "The Wilson Report," 25.

16. Ibid., 1.

17. Ibid., 3.

18. Ibid., 13.

19. Ibid., 20.

3. VARSITY JACKETS AND LETTER SWEATERS

1. Peter Brewington, "Neb. Districts Target of Gender-equity Suit," *USA Today*, 9 June 1995, 7C.

2. Karen Diegmueller, "Inequities in Girls' Sports Programs in Neb. Alleged," *Education Week*, 19 April 1995, 3.

3. Brewington, "Neb. District," 7C.

4. Diegmueller, "Inequities in Girls' Sports," 3.

5. "For the Record," *USA Today*, 14 August 1995, 11C.

6. "More Students Taking Part in High-school Athletics," *NCAA News*, 25 September 1995, 5.

7. Diagnostic Research, Inc., "The Wilson Report: Moms, Dads, Daughters and Sports," (Wilson Sporting Goods, Co., River Grove, IL, 7 June 1988), 1.

8. Sandra Scott, "Women in Decision Making Roles: Revisited" (Paper presented at the 74th Annual Meeting of the National Federation of State High School Associations, Nashville, Tennessee, 27 July 1993, 2.

9. Ibid.

10. Ibid.

11. Ibid.

12. Ibid.

13. Ibid, 4.

14. Ibid.

15. Ibid, 4–5.

16. Ibid, 6.

17. Ibid

18. Ibid, 7–8.

4. TURF WARS

1. Tony Graham, "Monmouth College Men's, Women's Athletics Nearly on Same Level," *Asbury Park Sunday Press* (NJ), 26 February 1995, H13.

2. Ibid.

3. Ibid.

4. Ibid.

5. Ibid.

6. "1993–94 High-school Sports Participation," *NCAA News*, 1 February 1995, 2.

7. Chuck Neinas, "Purpose of Statute Lost When Focus Put on Proportionality," *USA Today*, 9 March 1995, 2C.

8. "Parting Shots," *Sporting News*, 5 December 1994, 35.

9. "Women's Sports Foundation Responds to AFCA Action," *NCAA News*, 1 February 1995, 2.

10. Laurie Priest, "Time to Play Fair with Resources," *NCAA News*, 17 May 1995, 5.

11. Ibid.

12. Douglas Lederman, "Men Get 70% of Money Available for Athletic Scholarships at Colleges That Play Big-time Sports, New Study Finds," *Chronicle of Higher Education*, 18 March 1992, A1.

13. Mike Zapler, "Protecting Men's Sports," *Chronicle of Higher Education*, 6 January 1995, A44.

14. Lederman, "Men Get 70%," A1.

15. "Most Division I Athletics Programs Are in Debt, Study Shows," *NCAA News*, 22 December 1993, 7.

16. Ben Brown, "Law Gives Women Their Fair Share," *USA Today*, 9 June 1992, 2C.

17. "Most Division I Athletics," *NCAA News*, 7.

18. "Representative Seeks Title IX Guidelines," *USA Today*, 26 July 1995, 3C.

19. Priest, "Time to Play Fair," 5.

20. "1993–94 High-School Sports," *NCAA News*, 2.

21. Debra E. Blum, "Brown Loses Bias Case," *Chronicle of Higher Education*, 7 April 1995, A38.

22. Douglas Lederman, "A Key Sports Equity Case," *Chronicle of Higher Education*, 5 October 1994, A51–52.

23. Michael Scott and Judith Jurin Semo, "Ruling Has Title IX Significance," *NCAA News*, 28 April 1993, 1.

24. P. David Pickle, "Brown Ruling Could Add Emphasis to Hearings," *NCAA News*, 5 April 1995, 1.

25. Scott and Semo, "Ruling," 1.

26. "Brown Settles Portion of Sex-Discrimination Suit," *NCAA News*, 3 October 1994, 5.

27. Nat Gottlieb, "Evening the Score," *Newark Star Ledger* (NJ), 30 March 1995, 1, 12.

28. Lederman, "Key Sports Case," A51.

29. Blum, "Brown Loses," A37.

30. "Brown Won't Back Down," *York Daily Record* (PA), 19 August 1995, 1B.

31. National Collegiate Athletic Association, *Achieving Gender Equity: A Basic Guide to Title IX for Colleges and Universities* (Overland Park, KS: NCAA, October 1994), 31–32.

32. "School Not Allowed to Eliminate Women's Gymnastics, Court Rules," *NCAA News*, 25 October 1993, 3.

33. Ibid.

34. National Collegiate Athletic Association, *Achieving Gender Equity*, 28–29.

35. Ibid., 31.

36. Debra E. Blum, "U. of Texas at Austin Settles Sex-Bias Suit by Doubling Women's Sports Opportunities," *Chronicle of Higher Education*, 28 July 1993, A33.

37. Carol Herwig, "Female Athletes Recount Discrimination at Gender-Equity Enforcement Hearing," *USA Today*, 24 June 1993, 12C.

38. "Michigan State AD Resigns," *USA Today*, 9 February 1995, 10C.

39. Paul McMullen, "Yow Blazing Trail in ACC," *York Dispatch* (PA), 16 August 1994, B4.

40. Carol Herwig, "NCAA Programs Hiring More Female Coaches, Administrators," *USA Today*, 29 June 1994, 12C.

41. McMullen, "Yow Blazing Trail," B4.

42. Carol Herwig, "Big Ten Gives Women's Sports a Boost," *USA Today*, 3 June 1992, 1C.

43. "SEC Tackles Equity Issue," *NCAA News*, 9 June 1993, 3.

44. Christine H. B. Grant and Mary C. Curtis, "Judicial Action Regarding Gender Equity," (University of Iowa, 14 September 1993), 18.

45. Ibid., 18.

46. "Elsewhere," *USA Today*, 12 May 1995, 15C.

47. "Denver Enhances Women's Program," *NCAA News*, 9 June 1993, 10.

48. "Governmental Affairs Report," *NCAA News*, 25 October 1993, 22.

49. "Briefly in the News," *NCAA News*, 2 August 1995, 3.

50. Ronald D. Mott, "States Growing More Involved in Gender Equity," *NCAA News*, 9 June 1993, 1.

51. Mott, "States Growing More Involved," 20.

52. Michael Hiestand, "Bank Makes Commitment to Women's Sports," *USA Today*, 16 November 1993, 3C.

53. "Budget Boosts Revenue Distribution in Division I," *NCAA News*, 16 August 1995, 1, 10.

5. SHOWTIME

1. Julie Deardorff, "Women's Basketball Finding Its Audience," *Morristown Daily Record* (NJ), 16 March 1994, B1, B3.

2. Richard M. Campbell, "Women's Basketball Attendance Climbs Again," *NCAA News*, 28 June 1995, 1, 12.

3. "TV Interest, Attendance up Again for Women's Championship," *NCAA News*, 6 April 1994, 9, 20.

4. "Tuned in Big Time," *NCAA News*, 12 April 1995, 13.

5. Ronald D. Mott, "Rising Stock," *NCAA News*, 21 June 1995, 11.

6. "Huskies Ink TV Deal," *NCAA News*, 5 July 1995, 3.

7. Maria Ahmann, "The Story of Marianne Stanley," *Coaching Women's Basketball*, October/November 1993, 30–34.

8. Ibid., 34.

9. "Jury Award for Howard Women's Basketball Coach Reduced," *NCAA News*, 2 October 1995, 6.

10. Raymond Fazzi, "Gender Bias: Pay's off at RU," *Sunday Home News* (Woodbridge, NJ), 6 February 1994, A1, A12.

6. BASKETBALL NOMADS

1. Charles Q. Finley, "Competitive Fires Still Burn Bright in 'The Blaze'," *Newark Sunday Star Ledger* (NJ), 13 February 1994, 38.

2. Mike Weber, "No Pro Women's League? Blazejowski Not Bitter," *Newark Sunday Star Ledger* (NJ), 27 February 1994, sec. 5, p. 8.

3. Finley, "Competitive Fires," 38.

4. Sandy Seegers, "Blazejowski Weathered the Storms," *Morristown Daily Record* (NJ), 28 February 1994, B1.

5. Valerie Lister, "Courting Women's Pros," *USA Today*, 28 June 1995, 3C.

6. "Hoop Dreams," *USA Today*, 28 September 1995, 3C.

7. "American Basketball League," *USA Today*, 28 September 1995, 13C.

8. "Hoop Dreams," *USA Today*, 3C.

9. Debbie Becker, "Top Women Eye Shot at Atlanta," *USA Today*, 18 May 1995, 7C.

10. Debbie Becker, "Changes Give U.S. Women's Hoops Hope," *USA Today*, 15 December 1994, 1C.

11. Debbie Becker, "Edwards Makes Cut for National Team," *USA Today*, 26 May 1995, 14C.

12. Debbie Becker, "McClain Puts Team before Big Salary," *USA Today*, 23 May 1995, 3C.

7. THE PROFESSIONAL DILEMMA

1. Nancy J. Kim, "Mahwah Tournament a Showcase for Sponsors," *Record* (Hackensack, NJ), 13 July 1994, C1, C2.

2. "Unequal Pay," *USA Today*, 4 October 1995, 3C.

3. "USA Snapshots: Making a Million on Tour," *USA Today*, 25 February 1994, C1.

4. Richard Vega, "A Troubled Year for Women's Tennis," *USA Weekend*, 27–29 August 1993, 5.

5. Doug Smith, "Corel Corp. Logs on as WTA Tour Sponsor," *USA Today*, 12 October 1995, 1C.

8. THE LAST MALE BASTION

1. James S. Kunen and S. Avery Brown, "Sportswriter Lisa Olson Calls the New England Patriots out of Bounds for Sexual Harassment," *People Weekly*, 15 October 1990.

2. Ibid.

3. Ibid.

Selected Bibliography

Diagnostic Research, Inc. "The Wilson Report: Moms, Dads, Daughters and Sports." Wilson Sporting Goods, Co., River Grove, IL, June 1988, 7–15, 20–30.

Grant, Christine H. B., and Mary C. Curtis. "Judicial Action Regarding Gender Equity." University of Iowa, September 1993, 2, 3, 6, 9, 11, 12, 13, 15, 18–19.

National Collegiate Athletic Association. *Achieving Gender Equity: A Basic Guide to Title IX for Colleges and Universities.* Overland Park, KS: NCAA, October 1994, 39.

New World Decisions. "Miller Lite Report on Women in Sports." Miller Brewing Company, Milwaukee, WI, December 1985, 3–4, 6–7, 9, 12.

Scott, Sandra. "Women in Decision Making Roles: Revisited." Paper presented at the 74th Annual Meeting of the National Federation of State High School Associations, Nashville, Tennessee, July 1993.

Women's Sports Foundation. "Miller Lite Report on Sports and Fitness in the Lives of Working Women." Miller Brewing Company, Milwaukee, WI, 8 March 1993, 2, 4, 6, 11–15.

REFERENCE SOURCES

Ladies Professional Golf Association. *1994 Player Guide.* Daytona Beach: The Ladies' Professional Golf Association, January 1994, 4–5, 21–23.

Reith, Kathryn M. *Playing Fair: A Guide to Title IX in High School and College Sports.* New York: Women's Sports Foundation, 1992, 3–30.

Women's Tennis Association. *Official 1994 WTA Tour Media Guide.* St. Petersburg, FL: WTA Tour Players Association, January 1994, 8–9, 87, 133–34, 201–2, 247–48, 297–98, 358–79.

Index

About the Author

DAVID F. SALTER has been involved in athletics from tee-ball to inter-collegiate football. He was a journalist for ten years and is currently Director of Public Relations for York College of Pennsylvania. His first book, *Blueprint for Success*, analyzes Division I athletics.

ly
as